Greatest Naval Battles in History

My choice of the Fifteen most consequential Naval Battles in history

Nehal Kaur

Dedication

With profound reverence, this volume is warmly dedicated to my beloved grandmother, the inaugural storyteller who gently wove historical narratives into my world. Her tales, transcending mere recollections, blossomed as seeds of inspiration within me, kindling an impassioned quest to explore the rich, layered annals of history. Her stories, whispered from a place of wisdom and experience, became a bridge to bygone eras, igniting a flame that illuminated my path through the intricate mazes of the past.

Moreover, this work is a heartfelt homage to the historians, scribes, and translators spanning across nations and epochs, who have generously bestowed upon us a legacy, rich and enlightening, enabling our journey through the magnificent tapestry of human history. These dedicated individuals, through their scrupulous writings and meticulous preservation of manuscripts, have safeguarded the threads of our collective past, allowing us to weave them into our present and future narratives. Their endeavors, often crafted in the silent alcoves of contemplation and research, have illuminated our path through history, and to them, we extend our deepest respect and eternal gratitude. May this work echo their diligence and stand as a testament to the unbreakable chain of stories that link us all through time.

CONTENTS

Acknowledgement

The reflections, insights, and knowledge articulated within these pages are deeply rooted in the wisdom and stories generously shared by my grandmother. Her narratives have not only shaped my understanding of history but have also kindled a flame of curiosity and reverence towards our collective past.

A heartfelt acknowledgment is extended to the British Broadcasting Corporation (BBC), whose enthralling history documentaries have been a staple of my childhood and a pivotal source of inspiration. The compelling storytelling and meticulous research evident in their productions ignited my desire to delve into the study of history and explore the myriad of books that have informed this work, many of which are cited in my bibliography.

A sincere thank you to all the authors and scholars mentioned therein. While I may not have traversed the entirety of your work, I have endeavoured to ensure that any direct quotations have been duly credited. Your contributions to the field have been instrumental in shaping this book and the broader understanding of our shared history.

I would also like to acknowledge KDP on this occasion, after over 50 years of being a sponge for all things historic, I have been prolific in recent months since discovering this platform. I had given up on the idea of ever publishing any of my half-finished manuscripts with a feeling of resignation that writing and publishing was the preserve of the well to do, and independently wealthy, so thank you KDP.

Introduction and Honorable Mentions

"Great Naval Battles of History" takes readers on a chronological journey, delving into the turbulent waters of the most pivotal naval conflicts in history. This book is not simply a narrative of naval wars but rather an examination of how these conflicts have had a profound impact on the direction of history, impacting naval tactics, economic paths, and the destiny of nations.

The book's choice of the top 15 naval engagements was determined based on their influence on both immediate tactical outcomes and long-term strategic and economic ramifications. The selection of these conflicts was based on their significant impact on naval combat, their contribution to defining the geopolitical landscape, and their enduring influence on maritime history.

Nevertheless, prior to examining these monumental confrontations, it is crucial to recognise the notable mentions:

The Korean Joseon Kingdom's navy, under the command of Admiral Yi Sun-sin, engaged the Japanese navy in the Battle of Myeongnyang on October 26, 1597, in the Myeongnyang Strait, close to Jindo Island, off the southwest corner of the Korean peninsula. Admiral Yi defended the strait as a "last stand" battle against the Japanese navy, who were sailing to support their land army's push into the Joseon capital of Hanyang (modern-day Seoul), with only 13 ships remaining from Admiral Won Gyun's catastrophic defeat at the Battle of Chilchonryang.

It's uncertain how many ships the Japanese fleet actually had that Admiral Yi battled; Korean accounts put the number between 120 and 133 in combat, with up to 330 ships missing out altogether (312 overall). All accounts suggest that the Japanese ships vastly outnumbered the Korean ships, at least ten to one, regardless of the size of the Japanese fleet. Throughout the conflict, 31 Japanese vessels were either sunk or severely damaged. Amidst the conflict, numerous Japanese navy commanders lost their lives, including Tōdō Takatora. Overall, the Japanese suffered a humiliating naval defeat. Regretfully, I have had trouble locating any reliable sources for this conflict.

The Battle of the Downs (1639), The Battle of the Sound (1658), The Battle of Sicily (1676), The Battle of Suffren (1782), The Battle of Copenhagen (1801), The Glorious First of June, and The Battle of Navarino Bay. Each of these battles, albeit not achieving a position in the top 15, demonstrated the courage and expertise of the fighters engaged. Their exclusion from the primary roster does not decrease their importance but rather underscores the profusion of crucial maritime conflicts throughout history.

As the author, I acknowledge that there is a certain level of subjectivity involved in the selection process. The enormous scope of naval history offers a multitude of conflicts to select from, each possessing distinct strategic significance and tales of heroism. This book is written as an homage to all the conflicts, whether they are mentioned or not, and as a recognition of the challenge of selecting a limited number of historical events from such a vast array.

This book tries to offer the reader a full overview of the tactical, strategic, and economic ramifications of the selected naval wars. Each chapter delves deeply into the essence of naval warfare, exploring the strategic brilliance exhibited by admirals, the brave endeavours of sailors, and the significant ramifications of these engagements.

While exploring these pages, we will observe the progression of naval strategies, the rise of innovative technologies, and the astute strategic decision-making that shifted the outcome of conflicts. These wars are not merely individual occurrences; they are segments within the broader narrative of human striving, aspiration, and the unwavering quest for supremacy over the oceans.

Embark on this expedition through the tides of history, where every conflict unravels not only as a confrontation between naval forces but as a crucial turning point that influenced the world as we currently perceive it. "Great Naval Battles of History" is not just a book but rather an homage to the unconquerable determination of those who engaged in combat on the open waters and a memorial to the conflicts that shaped the course of maritime history.

This analysis of "Great Naval Battles of History" centres on the more recent period, examining the turbulent waters of naval warfare from the Renaissance to the present day. The ancient and antiquity periods, which are characterised by a diverse range of maritime conflicts, are specifically covered in a separate and devoted volume. In this exploration, we delve into significant conflicts that have profoundly influenced the contemporary world, ranging from naval artillery exchanges during the Age of Sail to the technical progressions of the 20th century. This book seeks to elucidate the strategic, political, and personal aspects that have characterised naval combat in contemporary times.

1. Leyte Gulf 1944 (15th place)

The Japanese Empire was eroded away inch by inch, and it is arguable that their High Command, by adopting the same concept as their ally Hitler in refusing to voluntarily cede ground once it was taken, did a great deal to lose the war for themselves. Without a doubt, Russia and the Western Allies, which included the United States of America and Great Britain, gained valuable insights from the challenging experience of being pushed back, and they took advantage of the shorter communications that were a compensation for withdrawal.

The American navy in the Far East believed that it was strong enough to launch an assault on the Philippine Islands by the autumn of 1944, when Anglo-American forces had firmly established themselves in Continental Europe. Japan places a high priority on protection and defence. A retaking of Luzon, the most northern island, by the United States would not only pose a direct danger to the Japanese home islands, but it would also be essential to the future course of the war because they have a supply route that goes through the South

China Sea. This was their oil pipe, and already their navy and their industries in general were beginning to suffer the effects of a severe shortage of this commodity, which is necessary to the conduct of battle at sea. As a result of the fact that American submarines had already lost a significant number of tankers, not only was it impossible for Japan to amass gasoline supplies, but it was also challenging to locate oilers for the Fleet Train at times.

When the navy went on a mission at a faraway location, this had the effect of limiting its mobility and affecting the question of where its base was located. At the end of August 1944, the United States began extending its air strikes to the Philippine Group for the very first time. This event is considered to be the prelude to the Leyte Gulf fight, which is considered to be one of the most complex marine battles that have ever ensued. There were attacks on the solitary islands of Chichi Jima and Iwo Jima, the first of which was barely 500 nautical miles away from Tokyo, as well as on Mindanao, which is the largest island in the southern region of the Philippines.

On September 10, surface forces closed the shore and destroyed a convoy of thirty-two small cargo ships. This was a direct result of the success that surface forces had achieved. In the short period of time following that, lodgements were established in the islands of Palau, to the east of Mindanao, and in Ulithi Atori. The primary advance base was going to be Ulithi, which is located 850 miles east of Leyte Gulf. Once the Americans had established a strong foothold in the Philippines, Ulithi was going to act as the primary forward base. On the fifteenth day of September, five days after the initial triumph against the convoy, it was decided to completely bypass Mindanao.

The Fleet had already gained valuable experience in this kind of operation in both the Mediterranean and the Pacific, so in October, they planned to launch an assault on Leyte with help from carrier-borne aircraft. The use of four divisions would be carried out, with Admiral Kincaid providing backup in the form of battleships, cruisers, destroyers, and escort carriers. During this time, the large fleet of carriers serving under Admiral Halsey carried out a number of missions over Formosa. From this location, Japanese aircraft that were based on land on the island were able to conduct operations over Luzon. Over the course of six days, the Japanese suffered the loss of well over 600 aircraft at the cost of going American. As a result of their counterattack, the Japanese were able to achieve some level of success; nevertheless, they misjudged the extent of the damage.

The advanced units of Admiral Kincaid landed commandos on Suluan Island in the Leyte Gulf on October 17th. The following day, they landed commandos on Dinagat and Homonhon, which are two islands located around 45 miles to the seaward of the major beaches of Leyte Island itself. Following a strong bombardment that began at ten o'clock on the morning of October 20th, the primary attack began, and for once, the local opposition was quickly defeated. But by this point, the Japanese navy had already responded with a powerful response. Kurita was the admiral who held the responsibility of destroying Kincaid. He proceeded to make his approach from a fueling facility located in North Borneo, but by the time he was prepared to set sail, the Americans had already successfully completed their landing.

However, even if he were to completely destroy Kincaid's fleet, the American situation would be extremely precarious, if not downright hopeless. This would be especially true if Kurita were successful in destroying the supply and supporting ships. Kurita possessed a significant amount of strength. He had twelve heavy cruisers, including the Atago, aboard which he flew his flag, and nineteen destroyers. He also had two enormous battleships, the Tamato and the Mushashi, as well as three older battleships, the Magato, Kongo, and Haruna. To get to the Leyte Gulf, Kurita would travel through the Mindora Straits and the Situyan Sea until he reached the San Bernardino Straits. From there, he would make a turn to the south and head in the direction of the Leyte Gulf. At the same time, a detachable force serving under Admiral Nishimura would approach Leyte from the southern direction.

Land-based air assistance would be provided because the remaining carrier power that Japan possessed would be with Admiral Ozawa, whose fleet was given the order to embark from Japan. In a short amount of time, the conflict transformed into a struggle for the safety of the Philippine landings and the survival of Kincaid's force. Admiral Halsey, who was working for Admiral Nimitz (Kincaid was in General MacArthur's sphere), had his entire fleet drawn to the north by Admiral Ozawa's magnet.

Despite the fact that his instructions covered the actions that Kincaid was concerned with, they included the following sentence: "In the event that the opportunity to destroy a significant portion of the enemy fleet is presented or can be created, such destruction becomes the primary task." Moreover, Halsey was of the opinion that Ozawa posed the most significant danger. Submarines from the United States did the first blood draw. There was a shadow cast over Kurita, and two cruisers were struck, one of which was the flagship

Atago, which unfortunately sank. Following that, the Mayo sank, and the Takao sustained damage. Kurita made the transition to a destroyer and then later to the large Tamato, and he continued his journey towards Leyte in accordance with the plan. Halsey had initially moved in towards the Philippines in three groups, with the moves directed at Leyte, the San Bernardino Straits, and Luzon. This was done in response to the reports that were received from the submarines. Additionally, carriers launched attacks against Kurita, who had lost the Mushashi as a result of an air raid.

However, Halsey was concerned by the lack of Japanese carriers, and he believed that Kurita had been crippled and had turned tail. As a result, he reorganised his troops and proceeded north in order to confront the possibility of a carrier threat. In addition to informing Kincaid of his movements, he shared his view that Kurita had sustained significant damage and was potentially retreating. According to the facts, the situation was as described below: Indeed, the northern force of Ozawa, which consisted of one large carrier, three light carriers, two battleships, three cruisers, and ten destroyers, was making its way towards Japan, but it was significantly lacking in aircraft and even less so in pilots who had received proper training. In spite of strikes and damage, Kurita was moving at twenty knots towards the San Bernardino Straits with four battleships, six heavy cruisers, two light cruisers, and ten destroyers.

This was the true menace that was coming from Kurita. Nishimura was also approaching with surface forces that included two battleships. In response to this twin danger, Kincaid had six battleships, eight cruisers, and approximately thirty destroyers. These battleships were ancient and equipped for bombardment rather than fleet engagement, and a significant amount of their ammunition had been expended. He designed and armed his unarmed and small escort carriers for troop and convoy assistance, not for fleet engagement. His escort carriers were also modest.

On the night of October 24–25, when Halsey was away from Leyte in order to meet with Ozawa, Kurita was getting closer and closer to the most important part of the invasion. Admiral Kincaid's dispositions had been based on the idea that the main onslaught would come from the south, from the Surigao Straits, which Nishimura would be approaching, and he recognised that there was no need to glance over his shoulder. They dutifully appeared before both Nishimura and a second independent force under the command of Admiral Shima, but they were both attacked and destroyed. The cruiser Mogami, which had been lucky enough to survive Midway, was one of the ships that went down in the conflict.

When the Leyte covering forces were dealing with Nishimura and Shima at daylight on October 25th and Halsey was 300 miles away looking for Ozawa, Kurita was steaming down the east side of Samar towards Leyte, his presence unnoticed. Halsey was searching for Ozawa. When he had made his way through the San Bernardino Strait in the dark, he had every opportunity to not only surprise Kincaid but also to inflict such a defeat that it may have put the entire invasion in jeopardy. Kurita made the discovery of Kincaid's northern group of escort carriers at 6:45 in the morning. Operating approximately forty miles out to sea, its primary mission was to offer support for the forces stationed on land. In the northern and centre groups, there were six carriers, whereas in the southern group, which was approximately one hundred twenty miles away, there were only four carriers.

As of this moment, the northern carriers were under the command of Rear-Admiral C. A. F. Spraguc, the centre carriers were under the command of Rear-Admiral Stump, and the southern carriers were under the command of Admiral T. L. Spraguc, who was in general command under Kincaid. Kurita was shocked, as well, because he had not anticipated coming across any carriers so far away from the Gulf of Mexico. This was the reason why he surprised the Americans. Consequently, he came to the conclusion that Kincaid's force must be a component of Halsey's primary fleet. As for the escort carriers, they believed that they were well protected to the north by forces that had, in fact, been concentrating on Halsey at that time. However, they did not have any patrols in the direction of Kurita's approach, and the first time they became aware of the enemy was at seven in the morning, when the Japanese battleships began firing their weapons.

The older type of capital ship was in the visible range of a carrier for the very first time, which was an extremely rare occurrence. According to the theory, the life of even a large carrier in the face of gunfire of battleship calibre should have been very short indeed. After receiving assistance from the reckless bravery of his light surface escorts and the airmen under his command, Rear Admiral C. A. F. Sprague retired in an easterly direction, into the wind, with everything on board flying. After that, the carriers progressively rounded to the south and south-west while under smoke, and beginning at 7.30 a.m., the escort, which consisted of seven tiny ships that were all lacking torpedoes, pressed home an attack in the face of intensive fire.

There was a remarkable level of success on the defensive side. Kurita's line of battle was temporarily disorganised as a result of the damage sustained by the cruiser Kumano.

Although Kurita had lost three of the escorts, he took a moment to gather his thoughts. It was his hesitancy that ultimately cost him the day, as he was subjected to an incredible succession of assaults from Hellcats and Avengers hailing from all three carrier groups, with Stump's being the first to arrive before the others. It was the aircraft that went in with everything they had; the torpedoes were short, and the bombs were not ideal for attacks on ships; in fact, several of the planes had nothing more powerful than machine guns. Admiral Kurita became convinced that he was in the face of a powerful carrier force as a result of his bravado, which resulted in the crippling and sinking of two of Kurita's cruisers. After two hours of firing, during which he had only succeeded in sinking one eight-knot carrier, the Gambler Bay, he recalled his forces and stood to the north. This occurred around nine twenty in the morning. He did this, and as a result, he was able to intercept a transmission in plain language that ordered aircraft to land and refuel on an airstrip in Leyte.

Additionally, he was able to lose one more cruiser to what was essentially an improvised air attack. Soon after lunchtime, Kurita made the decision to retreat from the region because he had visions of attacks by squadrons that were based on the coast. It was a very busy day for the escort carriers on October 25, 1944. Not only did they have to deal with the bombardment of battleships and cruisers, but at eight in the morning, when the situation with the northern group was extremely important, the Japanese air commander at Manila made the decision to send in suicide strikes by land-based aircraft. This organisation was known as the Kamikaze (Divine Wind) Corps. The term "Kamikaze" refers to the typhoon that occurred in the year 1281 and was responsible for the destruction of two ships that Kublai Khan had dispatched from Korea and South China to attack Japan. Four out of five kamikazes opened fire on the southern group, resulting in the destruction of two carriers. Both were able to live, but one of them ended up suffering more damage from a submarine torpedo a few moments later.

At that point, it was the turn of the northern force, which had just escaped from Kurita; however, the naval battle of Leyte Gulf had now come to an end. The consequences of the Naval Battle of Leyte Gulf, which took place between October 23 and October 26, 1944, had significant and long-lasting effects on the development of World War II, particularly in the Pacific Theatre of Operations. Not only did this fight, which was one of the largest naval conflicts in history, change the strategic landscape, but it also had huge economic and military ramifications for the parties involved in the conflict.

The Imperial Japanese Navy suffered a devastating defeat as a result of this battle. In addition to the deaths of hundreds of skilled sailors and aviators, Japan's naval capabilities were severely hampered as a result of the loss of four aircraft carriers, three battleships, and several other warships. Consequently, Japan was unable to conduct large-scale offensive naval operations as a result of this decision, which ultimately ended the country's capacity to project power across the Pacific. Due to the fact that the Japanese Navy's plan of deploying 'decisive battle' tactics was made outdated, they were forced to rely on increasingly desperate means such as kamikaze assaults. Japan was already in a fragile economic state, but the fight made it even more difficult. As a result of the cutting off of maritime channels, important resources, particularly gasoline and raw materials that were essential for the production of war goods, became extremely scarce, which further hampered Japan's efforts to compete in the war.

The United States-led Allied forces, on the other hand, were able to gain a lot from their victory in terms of both economic and strategic matters. In order to liberate the Philippines, which in turn damaged Japan's supply lines and weakened its capacity to sustain its forces in Southeast Asia, the effective defence of the Leyte Gulf was a critical factor because it was a key factor in liberating the Philippines. The Allies were able to strengthen their control over the Pacific as a result of this victory, which opened the door for additional offensives against Japanese-held territories.

The Allies were able to start the process of rebuilding the region's infrastructure and trade routes after the liberation of the Philippines, both of which had suffered significant damage during the war. This was a significant economic achievement. This was not only beneficial to the economics of the surrounding areas, but it also supplied strategic locations from which the Allies could launch additional operations. When it comes to the history of the military, the Battle of Leyte Gulf is frequently considered to be a pivotal moment in the history of naval warfare.

Consequently, it ushered in a new age in naval strategy and tactics, highlighting the significance of air power and the dwindling role of classic battleships. During the course of the Pacific War, the United States and its allies gained a major edge that they would use to their benefit in the later stages of the conflict. At the same time, the outcome of the battle imposed severe constraints on Japan, virtually erasing it as a naval force. In light of this, the victory at Leyte Gulf serves as a tribute to the strategic and tactical skill of the Allied forces, and it represents a crucial milestone on the way to triumph in the Pacific. The United States' naval might in the Pacific progressively pushed the Japanese back to their home waters, and this victory insured that the Philippines would be retaken by the United States.

2. Chesapeake Bay, 1781 (14th place)

Chesapeake Bay was thrilling victory the forces fighting for Independence, and must have had a demoralising effect on the British, Jones's triumph did not make any difference in the outcome of the situation. The independence of the United States of America was accomplished by the efforts of the American people, the brilliance of George Washington, the assistance of friends in France and Spain, and the utilisation of naval strength, which was not carried out by raiding squadrons but rather by fleets. Inconclusive combat that took place in Chesapeake Bay between Admiral Graves and the Comte de Grasse was the event that had the most significant impact on the outcome of the war and provided the most significant contribution to the formation of American destiny.

The event took place on September 5, 1781, which was over two years after the Serapis had brought her colours down off the coast of Yorkshire. In the context of the military, the turning point of the conflict occurred in 1777, following the battle of Saratoga. This was the moment when a British army that was attempting to march from Canada via the Hudson Valley to New York City was forced to surrender. Benjamin Franklin was able to finally bring the pact that he had been working on for such a long time to a successful conclusion when the news reached France.

From this point on, Washington would receive assistance from French regulars. On the high seas, squadrons would pose a threat to the British navy, both in its own waterways and in additional waters further afield. The British launched an attempt to take control of Virginia in the year 781. By this point, Cornwallis, the general commanding, had accomplished a great deal and appeared to have completed the more challenging portion of his campaign. After reaching the large inlet of the Chesapeake, he anticipated that he would be able to regain contact with the rest of the United States of America that was under British control by gaining control of the sea.

At the time of Graves's battle, Cornwallis was lying with his seven thousand troops at York Town, which is located on the York River, which runs into Chesapeake Bay. Although he was under siege on the landward side, he was not too uncomfortably positioned. The arrival of a British fleet was something he eagerly anticipated with self-assured anticipation. At the beginning of the year, the naval situation had been beneficial to the forces that were under the command of George III. During this time period, the West Indies were home to the principal French and British fleets, which were led by the Comte de Grasse and Admiral Rodney, respectively. There was a French squadron under de Barras that was based north of it, in Rhode Island, and there was a lesser division that was based in New York. Earlier in the year, armies from New York and Rhode Island engaged in a fruitless conflict off the coast of Cape Henry.

Following this, the French retired to Newport, leaving the British in command of the waterways in the area. The French government had already declined to provide means for a formal siege of New York, so de Grasse informed the generals that he would make for Chesapeake Bay. Washington and Rochambeau, the French general with whom he was operating, sent word to de Grasse that they hoped the next effort would be directed against either New York or the Chesapeake. However, de Grasse told the generals that he would make for Chesapeake Bay. In fact, this would have been the option that the military commanders would have chosen to go with. In an effort to conceal his plans, De Grasse assembled every ship that was available and made sure to travel through the Bahama Channel, which was not very busy at the time.

Twenty-four ships of the line were present when he

anchored in Lynnhaven Bay on the 30th of August. This bay is located just within the capes of the Chesapeake. In order to avoid coming into contact with the British, the fleet in Newport, Rhode Island, which consisted of eight ships of the line, four frigates, and transports, all of which were under the command of de Barras, set off for a rendezvous with de Grasse three days earlier. A push towards the head of Chesapeake Bay was led by Washington and Rochambeau, and it took place on August 24th. The movement involved crossing the Hudson River. A convergence of land and sea forces, all of which were unseen, was approaching Cornwallis.

In each and every respect, the British were terrible luck. In response to the news that de Grasse had left, Rodney dispatched fourteen ships of the line under the command of Admiral Hood to provide additional support to Graves in North America. Meanwhile, Rodney himself returned to England due to his poor health. Hood arrived at the Chesapeake three days before de Grasse, inspected the harbour, and upon discovering that it was devoid of any inhabitants, he continued on to New York. Despite the fact that Hood's force was the more powerful one, Graves was there to greet him. Due to the fact that Graves was the senior commander, he assumed command of the fleet.

The 31st of August was the day he set sail for the Chesapeake, with the intention of capturing de Barras before he could join de Grasse. Nineteen ships were under his command at the time. When Graves arrived at the Chesapeake, he was taken aback by the sudden appearance of a fleet that, judging by its size, could only have belonged to an adversary. At the very least, he had anticipated de Barras and, at the very least, an empty anchorage. Despite not being a tactical genius, Graves was a courageous individual, and according to his understanding of the situation, he was fully aware of the imminent threat that Cornwallis would face if de Grasse were not either beaten or at the very least forced to retreat. Due to the fact that he was in formation, he had the advantage of the wind.

At the time of the sighting, the French fleet was disorganised, and some of the ships were really making their way around Cape Henry. As Graves had for his second-in-command an officer of the brilliance of Samuel Hood, it could have been a wonderful day. A Hawke or a Howe would have undoubtedly flown the signal for a general chase, depending on the circumstances. In fact, a pursuit was most likely the only means that may have been capable of driving de Grasse away from his position. Graves did in fact launch an assault, despite the fact that his strength was inferior to that of de Grasse's, who had twenty-four ships to nineteen. However, as Mahan pointed out, "his method betrayed his gallantry."

When he communicated to his divisional commanders, he did it in accordance with his formalist beliefs, which included the belief that there should be a regular line of battle, from van to rear, ship to ship. There is also Drake. Graves' strategies were ones that de Grasse would have anticipated and with which he was very familiar. The outcome was uncertain, as would have been anticipated, and Graves' operations were those that de Grasse was familiar with. The confrontation resolved itself into a cannonade in the ancient way of warfare, with little close fighting and no surprising actions.

The Frenchman was given valuable time to command his squadrons, and the battle resolved itself into a cannonade. Approximately four o'clock in the afternoon marked the beginning of the action, which lasted for approximately two hours and a half before being interrupted by the passing of the light. Graves's subordinates, including Le Sieur de Bougainville, de La Touche-Treville, and Le Sieur de Monteil, were quite as illustrious as those of De Grasse. According to the French account of the engagement, M. de Bougainville initiated the action with a very quick fire, and the ships that were in the line of battle participated in the battle in a sequential manner. Only the eight leading ships of the English line participated in the battle to any significant degree.

For the most part, the centre of their fleet and their rear held themselves at half cannon shot. The wind completely failed the nine ships that were the last in our line. The penalties would have been appropriate for a number of actions that were inconclusive, with the only significant success being the serious damage that was caused to the British ship Terrible, which would have required it to be sunk shortly after the fight. The following day, at a council of war, Graves made the decision that it would be too risky to attempt to re-engage because a number of his ships were more or less disabled. He also rejected Hood's suggestion of attempting to seize the former French anchorage by stratagem, which was an idea that Hood himself had previously implemented with remarkable success against the same adversary in the West Indies.

During this time, a wind from the north-east was blowing both fleets away from the location where the ground operations were taking place. They were off Albemarle Sound by the 9th of September, and the British made their first sighting of Cape Hattcras the next day. During the evening of the ninth, de Grasse was unable to maintain contact with his opponent and instead went back to the Chesapeake, which he arrived at on the eleventh. There, de Barras joined him in his endeavours. Graves went back to New York with Admiral Hood, a subordinate who was extremely dissatisfied with his position.

Hood's fate, as it was so frequently, was to serve under people who were less talented than himself. Before the events of September 5th, it was likely that the United States would achieve its freedom. After the fact, it was unquestionable. Graves was completely conscious of the gravity of his failure as well as the processes that led to its occurrence. After the battle, he sent a memorandum to his captains, stating that the Line Ahead was meant to be a means to a goal and not an end in itself, and that "the signal for battle should not be rendered ineffective by strict adherence to the former." This memorandum was delivered the day after the battle. An example would have been preferable to either a precept or a post-mortem, and the flagships of both Graves and Hood were positioned in the queue in such a way that, while they could anticipate exercising authority, they were unable to launch daring manoeuvres. The only thing that could have brought about victory was a daring movement. Graves received no official displeasure because he and his captains had adhered to the rules. However, he was dissatisfied because he was using an outdated formal system that had been in place for a long time and because his signal book was not faultless. It was impossible to attribute any bad behaviour to him. A little bit longer, Cornwallis and his men managed to hold out, but with de Grasse off-shore, there was only one problem that could have arisen.

On October 19, 1781, formal conditions of surrender were signed, and although the struggle continued for one more year, there were no serious military activities carried out during that time. At the moment that Cornwallis put down his arms, a band from the United Kingdom played the song "The World Turned Upside Down," and shortly after that, a wave of joy spread over the United States. According to the legend, the elderly doorkeeper of Congress passed away from happiness upon hearing the news. When it came to the emancipation of his country, Washington was the only man who understood the significance of sea power more than anybody else. He wrote to Lafayette that "in any operation" and that "under all circumstances, a decisive naval superiority is to be considered a fundamental principle and the basis upon which every hope of success must ultimately depend." He was referring to the fact that "in any operation," France had been the source of the material.

Following the conclusion of the Battle of Chesapeake Bay, which took place on September 5, 1781, the aftermath of the conflict had enormous and long-lasting repercussions, which greatly impacted the path that the American Revolutionary War took. The outcome of this naval combat, although not very vast in scale, was a significant factor in determining the fate of the British and American troops, and it had far-reaching implications for both the economy and the strategic situation. Following the loss of the British navy by the French fleet headed by Admiral de Grasse, there was a significant strategic impact that occurred in the immediate aftermath.

The defeat that occurred at Chesapeake Bay prevented the British from either withdrawing or strengthening the army that General Cornwallis had commanded at Yorktown. The following surrender of Cornwallis served as a significant turning point in the Revolutionary War, and this blockade played a significant role in that capitulation. The defeat of the British in Chesapeake Bay practically brought a stop to major military operations carried out by the British in the United States. This was due to the fact that it became increasingly apparent that the war was unwinnable in light of similar defeats and the growing support from the world community for the American cause. Economically speaking, the conflict had huge repercussions for both the United Kingdom and the newly formed United States of America. It was becoming increasingly difficult for Britain to bear the burdens of the war, both in terms of its resources and its finances, and the setback that occurred at Chesapeake Bay further added to these burdens. Additionally, the loss served as a signal to other European countries that the British naval superiority was deteriorating, which had wider-reaching ramifications for British trade and colonial ambitions all over the world.

The United States of America and its French allies obtained a significant advantage as a result of their victory at Chesapeake Bay. Not only did it improve morale, but it also strengthened French backing, which was essential in terms of both financial assistance and military assistance because of the situation. As a result of the triumph, the United States was able to acquire additional international recognition and support, which was essential for the nation's economic and political stability when it gained its independence. When it comes to the history of the military, the Battle of Chesapeake Bay is sometimes considered a classic example of the significance of naval force in influencing the result of land warfare. I t was a demonstration of how control of the water might have a dramatic influence on the course of events on land, an idea that would continue to drive military plans in the centuries that would follow. In the last phases of the war, the American forces were able to capitalise on the strategic advantage that they gained as a result of the outcome of the battle, which imposed significant constraints on the military strategy that the British employed in the United States.

The victory at Chesapeake Bay is therefore considered a pivotal point in the struggle for the independence of the United States of America. This win highlights the interdependence of naval and land wars within the larger fabric of political and military history. Because of their defeat at the hands of the squadron of the Comte de Grasse, the English were unable to maintain their local dominance of the sea during the final phase of the American War of Independence.

3. Tsushima, 1905 (13th Place)

When the navies of Japan and Russia engaged in the first full-scale sea battle of the current century, it turned out to be the holocaust that some students of naval affairs had anticipated it would be. The loss of the Russians was complete, and it is difficult to come up with anything else that could have been looked for. During the summer of 1905, there were some people who believed that an act of harsh justice had been carried out in the Straits of Tsushima. However, for those who were caught up in it, it had very little to do with the chain of circumstances that led to their unfortunate situation.

It was a combination of high policy and strategic incompetence that led to their deaths. As a result of the conclusion of the war between China and Japan in 1895, Japan, which was an island country with a maritime tradition, was in possession of a significant portion of mainland territory that had belonged to China. This included the Liao-Tung Peninsula and its dockyard at Port Arthur. Russia, China's northern neighbour along the borders of Manchuria and Mongolia, protested against the cession of Port Arthur, arguing that its permanent occupation by a foreign power would be a standing threat to the government at Peking. She intended to keep what she had won, but when the terms of the peace treaty were made known, Russia objected to the cession of

Port Arthur. During the demonstration, Germany and France joined in, and the three powers manoeuvred their squadrons in an easterly direction. Japan, in response to the threat, altered the provisions of the treaty and returned Port Arthur to Chinese authority.

When Russia sought and secured the right to build a railway across Manchuria to the port of Niu-Chwang and, furthermore, the right to garrison Port Arthur and to use it as a naval station, the Treaty had just barely been filled with ink when Russia made these requests. They watched the continued Russian provocation of Japan without being moved, and they were unaware of the quiet fervour with which Japan was building up her navy. European statesmen gasped at such blatant cynicism, but instead of actively protesting, they themselves joined in a scramble for pickings between China and the United States.

In February of 1904, Japan had the feeling that it was prepared to take action. Her flotillas swooped down on Russian ships that were resting on the roads outside of Port Arthur and wreaked havoc on them without first making a formal declaration of war for the conflict. It was a shock to the Russians. Even though they were ingenious, the use of defensive minefields proved to be a blessing in disguise. This is because on April 1st, Admiral Makharoff, who was rumoured to be the most skilled officer in the Russian navy, offered battle to Admiral Heihachirō Togo and the main Japanese fleet.

However, the Russian flagship itself hit a mine, and Makharoff sank along with her. After gaining an early lead, the Japanese continued their offensive by capturing the heights that surrounded the Russian camp and by bombarding ships that were stationary at anchor. In addition, Admiral Vitgeft was beaten and murdered when he led the Russians to sea for a second time in August with the intention of joining forces with the squadron at Vladivostock. The Russian Eastern Fleet was no longer effective, and in order to avoid being coerced into accepting a humiliating peace, the Tsar would have to dispatch his Baltic ships around half of the world in an effort to bring the balance back into place. Following the Russian decision, the saga of delay, false alarm, and complications that followed was a tragicomedy that the entire world followed with attention. Admiral Rojdestvensky, an officer who was fifty-six years old, had a temperament that was explosive and had a strong record of service in operations against the Turks some years before receiving command.

Each of his four newly constructed battleships — the Borodino, the Orel, the Alexander III, and the flagship Suvaroff — formed the nucleus of his fleet. In addition to these formidable units, which were each armed with four 12-inch guns and twelve 6-inch quick-firers and had a nominal speed of 18 knots, which the engineers were unable to maintain very often, a fleet-train consisting of a variety of older battleships, cruisers, torpedo boats, and a fleet-train that included everything from transports to hospital ships was also present. This was not a coherent fleet but rather a procession of vehicles.

At Reval, on October 9th, the Tsar conducted an inspection of the ships. It was one week later that Rozhestvensky arrived on the scene. He was perplexingly anxious from the very beginning. According to the reports, the Japanese were in possession of homemade torpedo ships that were intended to lie in wait in order to launch an attack against the Russians before they entered the Baltic Sea and the North Sea. During the early stages of his advancement, Rozhestvensky really opened fire on a Swedish merchantman and a German fishing boat. Additionally, an English fishing fleet that was located off the Dogger Bank was shocked to see that it was being attacked by the tremendous power of Russian naval forces. In the previous wars that took place off the Dogger, the British and Dutch had engaged in combat on several occasions; nevertheless, there had never been an engagement quite like this one!

However, a trawler was sunk, and a number of innocent lives were lost as a result of the Russian gunfire, which was horrible. Rozhestvensky divided his force upon reaching Tangier, which was being observed by a British squadron led by Lord Charles Beresford. After completing his own journey around Africa, he dispatched a division led by Admiral Felkersham to the Mediterranean Sea, with the directive that they take the path that went through the Suez Canal. During the month of December, Rozhestvensky completed a circuit of the Cape of Good Hope and then proceeded to Madagascar. He moored off the coast of Tamatave on New Year's Day in 1905, and it was there that he received the word that Port Arthur had surrendered.

It appeared that the admirals were not in a hurry to move forward, despite the fact that Rozhestvensky's and Felkersham's forces had reached a point of reunion. The enemy had control of their own nearby base, and the only thing they could hope to accomplish was to fight their way past Togo's fleet and arrive at Vladivostock via combat. There were hardly many people, even among the most upbeat Russians, who believed that they had a good chance of defeating the Germans on the crossing. The Russians did not leave the waters of Madagascar until the 25th of March, which put significant pressure on the French government's willingness to be friendly. As of the 8th of April, they were well out at sea and just off the coast of Singapore.

The ships that they were using were burning soft coal, and this tremendous cloud of smoke was trailing behind them from forty different boats, which included everything from battleships to colliers. Rozhestvensky received his final reinforcement in the ports of French Indo-China, where he spent the months of April and May. The following day, on May 14th, he set out on the last stage of his journey, which was the final step before the inevitable confrontation with the Japanese. In order to reach Shanghai, he travelled across the Bashee Channel, which is located between Formosa and the Philippines. When the battle ships arrived at that location on May 25th, they separated from the auxiliary ships that were anchored near the mouth of the Yangtze River.

In the evening of the same day, the admiral made his way to the Straits of Tsushima, which are the waterways that divide the island of Tsushima from Honshiu, which is the primary home island of Japan. It was a horrible day with a rising wind and cold rain, which created a haze that was so thick that it was blinding. The Russians were ecstatic about this fact because they had high hopes that it would confuse the enemy scouts. During the time that the Russians were on their lengthy journey, Togo had ample time to train his squadrons and flotillas, to refine ammunition that had been shown to be inadequate in prior conflicts, and to establish the finest dispositions that were possible.

He was quite close to his bases; he was familiar with every facet of the waterways in the area; and he had a hundred different reasons to be confident. His moves were just as obscure to the rest of the world as his country was to individuals. The only thing that people were aware of was that Rozhestvensky's prospects of winning were extremely low, regardless of how strong he would appear to be or how much more powerful he might be. When Togo realised that the Tsushima channel was the most likely path for Rozhestvensky, he designated Masampo Bay, which is located in South Korea, as the primary station for his fleet. It was from this location that he planned and executed his attack. Before the two long columns that the Russians advanced, there were three quick cruisers that were in front of them.

There was a cruiser and two destroyers stationed at the wing of each column. During the Suvaroff, Rozhestvensky himself led the more powerful starboard line. This line had four new battleships in addition to four others, making the total number of battleships eight. The port line consisted of eight ships, with the Rear-Admiral leading the way with the two major columns. Following the rear admiral were four storage ships, two repair ships, and two steamer medical vessels. Under his leadership, Togo was in charge of four battleships. A Japanese ship called the Siono Maru and an armed liner came dangerously close to colliding with one of the Russian hospital ships on May 27. The incident occurred in the early morning haze. With three cruisers serving as escorts, the Siano Maru communicated the location of the Russian fleet to the Togo.

The cruisers belonging to the Japanese navy were under the direction of Rear Admiral Dewa, and they maintained a course that was parallel to that of the Russian fleet at a distance of nearly five miles. It is believed that an officer in the Orel accidentally opened fire around 11.20, which resulted in the Russians opening fire. The message that Rozhestvensky sent was, "Ammunition is not to be wasted." The action came to a halt. "Change course north 23 degrees east for Vladivostock," the signal said at noon, when the Russians were located due south of Tsushima. On the occasion of the anniversary of the coronation of the Tsar, officers had gathered around the tables in the ward room and drank Imperial health in a serious manner. It was just before two o'clock when Togo caught a glimpse of his adversary, who was located to the south-west of the island of Okonoshima and to the east of Tsushima.

He sent a signal to his fleet, saying, "The outcome of today's battle will determine whether the Empire will rise or fall." Let every man reach his full potential. In the traditional fashion, he started his assault by "crossing the T" in a slight diagonal direction and at a distance of approximately 9,500 yards. This was exactly how he had meant to begin his assault. While this was going on, his cruiser squadrons were heading in the direction of the Russian flanks and rear. As a result of Togo's superior speed, he was able to turn around and recross Rozhestvensky's bows after he had already crossed them. Subsequently, Rozhestvensky manoeuvred his vessel in a parallel direction, and a general fight took place at a distance of up to five miles. Both the rapidity and accuracy of the Japanese fire were decisive factors in determining the outcome. 'After the first twenty minutes,' a Japanese officer reported, 'the Russians seemed to suddenly go all to pieces, and their shooting became wild and nearly harmless.' This was the beginning of the Russian attacks.

Approximately thirty minutes before three o'clock, the Suvaroff veered out of the queue with her steering inoperable, and from that point on, the struggle escalated into a merciless slaughter. The Russian battleships were taken out of action one by one, and by five o'clock, they were crowded together in a confused mob. Togo himself assaulted them from the east, and his cruisers attacked them from the south. Their confusion caused them to pack together. Despite the fact that she was incapacitated and on fire, Suvaroff was still flying her flag, even though she had already moved to the west. Additionally, Rozhestvensky had suffered two wounds, and his flag captain had been slain. The last instruction that he had given to Nebogatoff was to make an attempt to reach Vladivostock with at least a portion of the fleet. The sun went set, and with it, any last hopes that the Russians had vanished.

The destruction continued into the second day. Rozhestvensky, along with a handful of his officers, had transferred to a destroyer; however, she was intercepted by a Japaijese flotilla and taken captive on the afternoon of the 28th. There was just one tiny cruiser, the Almaz, and two destroyers that ever made it to Vladivostock. These were the only Russian ships that ever arrived there. It was a story that, in comparison to the one about the Armada of Philip II of Spain, appeared to be practically a triumph. As a consequence of the conflict, the Japanese resurrected the time-honoured practice of absorbing, repairing, and restoring some of their most prized captures into their own fleet. The only thing that they suffered was damage to their torpedo craft, and even the damage to their larger units was insignificant. Despite the fact that many Russians showed individual bravery, no victory had ever been more humbling or comprehensive as this one. She had demonstrated that she was capable of manoeuvring and training a fleet that was comparable to anything that was afloat. It is Japan's hope that over the course of the next 35 years, she will continue to strengthen her naval capabilities until the moment comes when she will be able to compete with the power and effectiveness of the United States.

The naval battle of Tsushima, which took place on May 27 and 28, 1905, between the fleets of the Russian and Japanese nations, had important repercussions and outcomes that transformed the strategic and economic landscapes of the early 20th century. An important turning point in naval warfare, this fight was a critical event in the Russo-Japanese War. It not only shifted the balance of power in East Asia, but it also had worldwide repercussions and marked a turning point in naval warfare.

There were immediate strategic repercussions that resulted from the overwhelming success that the Japanese achieved in the near term. It was extremely impossible for Russia to maintain its naval force in the Far East, and the country lost almost all of its fleet in the Pacific. This defeat compelled Russia to acknowledge that it was unable to continue the war, which ultimately resulted in the signing of the Treaty of Portsmouth on September 5, 1905. In accordance with the terms of the treaty, Russia handed over the sovereignty of Port Arthur, the South Manchurian railway, and the southern half of Sakhalin Island to Japan.

This marked the conclusion of the Great War between Russia and Japan. Japan became a powerful imperial power as a result of this change, which drastically shifted the balance of power in East Asia. The fight and the following treaty had significant repercussions for both countries by way of their respective economies. At a time when Russia was already struggling economically due to the costs of the war and internal upheaval, the country faced additional hurdles. The setback was a contributing factor in the growing discontentment among the Russian public, which would finally result in the Russian Revolution of 1905. The economic situation in Japan improved as a result of the victory and territorial gains, which allowed the country to gain access to vital resources and trade routes.

However, as a result of the war's overwhelming financial load, Japan is now heavily indebted, which has planted the seeds for future economic difficulties. The Battle of Tsushima was a significant event and a watershed moment in the history of the military. The win was the first decisive victory in the history of modern naval combat when an Asian state defeated a European force. It also served as a demonstration of the efficacy of modern naval strategies and technology, including the utilisation of superior gunnery and wireless communication. The conflict brought to light the significance of speed, firepower, and efficient command and control in naval warfare.

As a result, naval strategies and ship designs went through significant changes in the years leading up to World War I. The defeat imposed severe constraints on Russia's naval capabilities and worldwide ambitions, whereas the triumph gave Japan not only territory and economic rewards but also a huge rise in international prestige. Japan saw a significant boost in its international stature as a result of the win. As a result, the Battle of Tsushima is considered to be a pivotal moment in the annals of military history. It is a symbol of the beginning of a new age in naval warfare as well as the shifting tides of global power dynamics in the early 20th century. In this Japanese strait, Admiral Togo was responsible for the first major fleet action of the current century, which resulted in the complete destruction of the Russian fleet.

4. Pursuit of the Bismarck (12th Place)

In the early summer of 1941, after the Second World War had been going on for the better part of two years, Great Britain and her self-governing dominions discovered that they did not have any allies that were able to effectively support them. Both France and Britain's little army were pushed off the continent by the most effective and mobile conqueror since Napoleon. France was vanquished, and Britain gained control of the continent. During the night, her towns were subjected to aerial assault, and her navy was stretched to its limits, and in theory, it was stretched even further than that.

The United States of America was friendly but neutral, and Stalin, who was partial to Hitler's conquest of Germany at the time, boasted that he would not pluck any British chestnuts out of the fire. Despite the fact that Britain's duties at sea were global in scope, the Atlantic Ocean, which served as her lifeline, was at imminent risk of being cut off by a submarine blockade. It was known in May that the Bismarck, the most powerful man-of-war that had ever been constructed in Europe, was getting ready to go on her first voyage. As if all of this disaster were not enough, so to speak.

If she were to be able to escape into the Atlantic Ocean, she would be able to cause a great deal of damage to shipping, and the ports on the west coast of France would be ready to welcome her after her goal was satisfied. Together with the heavy cruiser Prinz Eugen, the Bismarck, which was flying the flag of Admiral Gunther Lutjens, set out from the Baltic Sea on May 8th. Air reconnaissance confirmed their departure, and it was believed that they were heading in a westerly direction. It was also anticipated that they would reach the Atlantic trade routes by means of the Denmark Straits, which are the strait that separates Greenland and Iceland.

On the 23rd of May, the British cruisers Norfolk and Suffolk were conducting patrols in that region. Both ships saw the Germans, with the Norfolk coming under fire at a range of six and a half miles and disengaging under the cover of smoke due to the fact that smoke was there. Admiral Tovey, who was in charge of the British Home Fleet at the time, went ahead and took the report that her captain had written. At that time, he was some 600 kilometres to the south-east. At full speed, Admiral Holland, who was closer to the location, shifted his attention towards the position. Holland's flag was flying on the battle-cruiser Hood, which was twenty-five years old but was considered to be powerful and equipped to the point where it could take on anything that was afloat by virtue of its capabilities.

She was accompanied by the battleship Prince of Wales, which had just recently been finished but had not yet been completely operational. With the British capital ships capable of travelling at speeds of no more than 28 knots and the Germans rated at 30, surprise was absolutely necessary in order to bring about an action, and Holland relied on Admiral

43

Wake Walker's two cruisers for guidance. Snowstorms caused Norfolk and Suffolk to temporarily lose contact with the Germans at a crucial stage in Holland's approach. This occurred during the critical stage. Holland, who was under the impression that this was owing to the fact that the adversary had changed their direction to south-cast, changed his own path from one of westerly intercepting to one of due north, reducing his speed to 25 knots.

On the 24th of May, at 2.47 in the morning, the Suffolk was able to regain communication, and it was then possible to plot the position and speed of the Bismarck. There was an increase in speed to 28 knots for the two large British ships, and at 4:30 in the morning, visibility had increased to twelve miles. The reconnaissance aircraft belonging to the Prince of Wales was getting ready to take off in order to provide Holland with the precise location of the enemy. However, the pilot discovered that his fuel had been tainted by sea water, and as a result, the machine was discarded. When the enemy came into sight at 5.35 in the morning, Holland intended to concentrate the fire of both of his ships on the Bismarck, leaving the Prinz Eugen to the Norfolk and Suffolk. However, when the fight began eighteen minutes later, the relative positions benefited the Germans.

When they were at a range of approximately thirteen miles, they were too close to the Hood's starboard bow for her two after-turrets to be able to engage in combat. On the other hand, the British were somewhat ahead of the beam and were consequently exposed to their full broadside. Rather than being able to open fire with the eight 15-inch guns of the Hood and the ten 14-inch guns of the Prince of Wales, Holland was only able to use the four forward 15-inch guns of the Hood and the five forward 14-inch guns of the Prince of Wales. This was due to the fact that one of the Prince of Wales' six forward guns was defective.

All eight of Bismarck's 15-inch guns and all eight of Prinz Eugen's 8-inch guns were available for Admiral Lutjens to use to their full potential. With Lutjens focusing his attention on the Hood, which was leading the British, all four ships opened fire simultaneously at a distance of around 26,500 yards. Assuming that the German ship was the Bismarck, Holland had given orders for both of his ships to concentrate their efforts on the left-hand German. The opposite was true. In a fortunate turn of events, the gunnery officer of the Prince of Wales changed the target for his own personal responsibility. The Prinz Eugen's 8-inch guns caused a fire near the main mast of the British flagship, which extended forward and flared high above the top deck. This occurred shortly after both German ships focused their attention on the Hood, which was the target of their attacks.

At 5:55, Holland issued an order to turn away from the adversary by twenty degrees. But as he was turning a salvo around the hood, flame leapt hundreds of feet, and her mighty form dissolved into a vast column of smoke. Out of this column of smoke, her bow and stern rose steeply as she broke amidships and disappeared beneath the sea. This would have brought the full broadsides of both of his ships to bear on whatever was going on. Her magazines had detonated as a result of the incoming shells, and the 'might, majesty, dominion, and power' that the ship represented had been destroyed in the same manner as three other vessels of her unfortunate type that had been destroyed at Jutland a quarter of a century earlier.

For the time being, the Germans were free to focus their attention on the Prince of Wales. It didn't take long for her to get into trouble. All of the men on her compass platform, with the exception of Captain Leach, were either killed or injured when a 15-inch shell struck it. Within a short period of time, she was struck no less than six more times, with two shells dropping on the water line aft, allowing 500 tonnes of water to enter the vessel. As one cannon after another failed to function properly, the builder's foreman, who was present, performed a tremendous amount of labour to rectify the issues. However, the Bismarck appeared to be in very good condition, despite the fact that the front salvoes of the ship averaged only three cannons rather than five guns. Captain Leach made the astute decision to halt the engagement until reinforcements could be called upon, but even as he moved away from the battle under the cover of smoke, the ships that were involved in the engagement jammed.

However, one of the last shots fired by the Prince of Wales was successful in hitting three targets. Lutjens made the decision to terminate his Atlantic mission as a result of the damage, which created a leak of oil fuel and led the Bismarck to decelerate somewhat. At this point, the Prince of Wales joined Norfolk and Suffolk in their efforts to shadow individuals. As they moved in a southwesterly direction, the Germans occasionally made an effort to dislodge the British. It was estimated that the earliest possible moment for this to take place was seven o'clock in the morning on May 25. Admiral Tovey, along with his primary fleet, was sailing at high speed to intercept, and they were around 300 miles away at this point.

During the afternoon of May 24 at 1.20 p.m., the Suffolk reported that the Germans had slowed down and had changed their course to the south-east. The prospects for the United Kingdom improved. Admiral Somerville and his Gibraltar force were called to the north, and every ship that was available was given the order to close to the coast. In light of the fact that it was not yet known for certain whether the Bismarck had sustained damage or was merely conserving gasoline, the airmen aboard the carrier Victorious, which was accompanied by Admiral Tovey, were requested to reduce the speed at which she was travelling. There were nine planes that took off from the carrier at ten o'clock at night on the day that the Hood was sunk. The weather was terrible, and the flight deck was rising and dropping by around fifty feet. It was pilots who had never flown off the deck of a ship before who were on their way to Malta and were in charge of the aircraft. As of 1:27, they were able to establish radar contact.

Attacks were pressed home against heavy antiaircraft fire in the most difficult conditions that could possibly exist. While one torpedo struck amidships, it did not cause any significant damage. There was a loss of two shadowing aircraft. In order to give the Prinz Eugen the opportunity to break away independently to the southwest, the Bismarck had turned to engage her surface reconnaissance vessels just a short time before this air strike. After that, the battleship once again set sail in a southerly direction. The subsequent incident took place in the early hours of May 25. It was then that the Suffolk, which had been keeping a close eye on the Bismarck for such a considerable amount of time, lost contact with it, possibly due to an excessive amount of self-assurance. Although there was a widespread belief that Lutjens must have turned to the west and that he was being pursued in that direction, the truth was that he had actually changed his course to the south-west and was heading in the direction of St. Nazaire.

The subsequent time period, which endured for a minimum of 31 and a half hours, was characterised by an increasing level of confusion. False reports that the Bismarck had turned north-east and was in the process of breaking back the way she had come forced Admiral Tovey to change her course, causing her to lose valuable distance. A Catalina aircraft belonging to the Royal Air Force Coastal Command was the next to make a sighting of Lutjens, which took place at 10.30 a.m. on May 26. After coming under severe fire, the aircraft's crew was able to submit a report that the battleship was around 690 miles north-west of Brest. They were travelling at a speed that would bring her under the shelter of U-boat patrols and the bombers of the Luftwaffe within twenty-four hours. At this point, a significant number of the searchers were running out of gasoline, and two ships, one of which was the Prince of Wales, were making their way back to port because of this.

At this point, it appeared that Admiral Somerville was in the best position to intercept, and his aircraft, which was flown from the Ark Royal, quickly located a ship and attacked her, despite the fact that visibility was extremely poor. It was fortunate that the airmen's aim was weak because she turned out to be the British cruiser Sheffield, which was located twenty miles north of the enemy at the time. At approximately 8.45 p.m., further strikes, which were also carried out in adverse weather conditions, were more successful. There were two torpedoes that struck.

In the right-aft direction, one of them smashed the steering gear of the Bismarck and jammed her rudders. Even though it took a few hours before the situation became clear, this damage would ultimately determine her fate. Over the course of the night of May 26th, five destroyers led by Captain Philip Vian, which had been separated from a convoy, made contact with the adversary and launched torpedo strikes. These attacks were successfully repelled by radar-controlled fire from the main batteries of the Bismarck. On the other hand, Vian's ships remained in the shadows throughout the night, and the next day, they brought the Bismarck to its destruction. On the morning of May 27th, at 8:46 a.m., the King George V, which was Admiral Tovey's flagship, began fire at a range of 16,000 yards, practically simultaneously with the Bismarck. HMS Rodney was sailing alongside Tovey, and the British Commander-in-Chief gave the captain of the Rodney permission to open fire and gave him the open command to do so. Gunfire continued until 10:15, at which point the Bismarck had been reduced to what appeared to be a shambles that was on fire.

Despite the fact that the German salvoes had stopped, the Bismarck's construction proved to be just as astounding as her offensive capacity, which was comparable to that of a fleet in the earlier days of steam warfare. Her belt armour remained unpierced, and neither shells nor torpedoes were able to penetrate her engine rooms, according to some of her survivors, despite the fact that she had been exposed to a great deal of pounding. When the turbine engineer-officer was given the order to blow the explosive charges in the sea valves, the majority of her machinery was still in working order. The two torpedoes that were fired by the cruiser Dorsetshire just sped up her disappearance and did not cause it. With the exception of the submarine, most of the different types of naval vessels that are currently in use were involved in the pursuit of the Bismarck.

Although she was being followed by cruisers, she was ultimately passed over by a battlecruiser and a battleship, which resulted in devastating consequences. Following the loss of contact, it was an aircraft that was responsible for re-discovering her, and the sea-borne air attack was responsible for major damage. It was the gunfire of battleships that ultimately determined the destiny of the Bismarck, while destroyers were responsible for maintaining night shadowing. The Prinz Eugen had fought her to the very end with the utmost bravery, and he had survived to see many more days of life go by. A decision that permitted two powerful German ships to enter Turkish waters during the First World War had a significant impact on the entire situation. The British had the intention of ensuring that a similar incident did not occur during the second conflict; however, it required the utilisation of all of their available resources, in addition to the loss of their most aesthetically pleasing ship and nearly all of her gallant company, in order to guarantee that the Bismarck and her consort did not add to the existing threat to the Atlantic life-line.

The chase of the German battleship Bismarck in May 1941, which ultimately resulted in its sinking, had important repercussions and effects, which had an impact on the strategic and economic aspects of World War II. Although it was not a conventional naval combat, this incident was a significant turning point in the naval warfare that was taking place during that time period. It had far-reaching repercussions for both the Allied troops and the German military. The loss of the Bismarck had a significant strategic impact on the ways in which Nazi Germany conducted its naval operations in the immediate aftermath of the event. With its status as one of the most powerful battleships of its era, the Bismarck played a pivotal role in Germany's naval strategy, notably with regard to the disruption of Allied transport lanes in the Atlantic.

The sinking of the ship not only resulted in a substantial loss of naval capability for the Germans, but it also dealt a tremendous blow to the morale of the German military, the Kriegsmarine. This defeat compelled Germany to re-evaluate its surface fleet operations, which resulted in a growing emphasis on submarine warfare, which would ultimately lead to an intensification of the Battle of the Atlantic. The demolition of the Bismarck was a huge success for the Allies, notably for the Royal Navy of the United Kingdom. During the war, it eliminated a significant danger to Atlantic convoys, which were essential for supplying and bolstering Britain's forces. Strategically speaking, this victory boosted the morale of the Allied forces and established their naval dominance as well as their ability to effectively coordinate a large-scale naval operation.

Due to the fact that planes from the HMS Ark Royal were instrumental in rendering the Bismarck inoperable, the victory also served to emphasise the significance of air power in naval warfare. In terms of the economy, the chase and sinking of the Bismarck alleviated some of the pressure that was being placed on the shipping lanes of the Allies, which were essential for ensuring that resources and supplies continued to flow. This loss was a setback for Germany in their efforts to cut off supply lines to Britain, which was a vital component of their strategy to damage the British war effort. Germany's objective was to weaken the British war effort. When viewed through the lens of military history, the event brought to light the fact that even the most formidable battleships are susceptible to the influence of air power, as well as the significance of information and reconnaissance in contemporary naval combat. As a result of the chase of the Bismarck, the naval strategy shifted away from typical battleship engagements and towards a concentration on aircraft carriers and submarines. In general, the sinking of the Bismarck allowed the Allies to gain a strategic and moral advantage while also imposing substantial constraints on the capabilities and strategies of the German navy.

This episode is remembered as a defining milestone in naval warfare, exemplifying the intricate interaction of strategy, technology, and intelligence that occurred throughout the maritime wars that occurred during World War II. Following the sinking of the British battle-cruiser 'Hood,' the Bismarck, which was the most powerful battleship that was afloat at the time, was chased and sunk in the Atlantic Ocean.

5. Flamborough Head, 1779 (11th Place)

Upon Paul Jones of the American ship Bonhomme Richard's remarkable victory over a British frigate in the autumn of 779, Great Britain had been at war with her North American colonies for more than four years. King George III's situation was dire, especially for his navy. His foes, France and Spain, were about to join him: Gibraltar was in danger, and the islands of Grenada and St. Vincent were prime targets for conquest. A man born thirty-two years ago in Kirkbean, Kirkcudbrightshire, the village that had given birth to John Campbell, Hawke's flag captain at Quiberon Bay, was to humiliate Britain even closer to home. John Paul Jones was the gardener's youngest surviving kid. An older brother had made his home in Virginia and was doing well there. John Paul Jones, who became known by his surname after dropping his initial Christian name and joining the American military, began learning to sail at an early age.

He worked as an apprentice on Whitehaven ships involved in the North Atlantic trade. Afterwards, he became a slave trader and eventually became the captain of a brigantine. Subsequently, he worked as a smuggler between the Isle of

Man and the Solway Firth. Paul Jones learned of his brother's death in Virginia in 1773 while trading in the West Indies. He then assumed management of the estate. He enlisted in the newly-forming revolutionary fleet two years later. His naval experience was extensive and varied, earning him a commission and a position as first lieutenant of a frigate with thirty guns. Shortly after, he gained autonomous command, initially of a sloop and subsequently of a recently constructed frigate, the Ranger, with which he was tasked with sailing to France. Paul Jones carried his ship to Brest, where he re-fitted after visiting Nantes, his first port of call.

He set out on a tour in April 1778 with the intention of harassing commerce in the Irish Sea as well as around the coastlines of Wigtown, Kirkcudbright, Cumberland, and the Isle of Man, which were some of his early haunts. While he caused much anxiety and inflicted some damage locally, his most notable achievement was defeating the Drake, a warship, in Belfast Lough. He returned to Brest on May 8th, well justified in his sense of pride. Although Paul Jones enjoyed great fame in France, his team harboured animosity towards him, leading to a steady defiance.

Jones finally relinquished his command, and he was out of a job until the following spring, when he managed to get the Due de Duras, an old French East Indiaman, berthed at L'Orient. In honour of his longtime friend Benjamin Franklin, whose book Poor Richard's Almanack had just been translated into French as La Science du Bonhomme Richard, he renamed her the Bonhomme Richard. With forty cannons on board, Jones's new vessel set out on August 14, 1779, carrying a complement of 380 men; around 150 of them were French volunteers. The others were mostly misfits from various nations. With Jones sailed the Alliance, an American-built frigate commanded by Pierre Landais, a Frenchman who had taken service under the American Government, the Pallas, a French frigate, and the Vengeance, small French ships also sailing under the Stars and Stripes.

Well handled, this could have been a formidable raiding squadron, but Jones, with all his gifts, did not possess the art of winning devotion, and from the first difficulties with his captains, with Landais in particular, were marked and serious. As early as 23 May, off the coast of Ireland, one officer and twenty men deserted from Jones's own ship, the Cerf parted company, never to re-appear, and little more was heard of the Vengeance. Jones then took his squadron up the west coast of Ireland, rounded the north of Scotland, and sailed down the east coast, where it was likely he would be able to capture valuable prizes. He was not disappointed.

Prizes came his way, but he found it increasingly difficult to keep his force together. Landais, with no tradition of discipline, regarded himself almost as an independent privateer and frequently made cruises on his own, paying no regard to the rendezvous which Jones had been careful to arrange. At one time, Jones made a show of force off Leith, spreading consternation in Edinburgh, but he was driven out of the Firth of Forth by a westerly gale. When it abated, he was far out to sea, and he decided that alarm and preparation would have destroyed his chances of success. Sensibly enough, he decided to attempt off the English coast what he had failed to do in the Forth.

By a fortunate chance he fell in with the Alliance, which had once more become separated, on 23 September, shortly before a large convoy, believed to comprise the Baltic trade, was sighted coming southwards round Flamborough Head. The merchantmen were under escort from the Serapis (Captain Pearson), a newly built frigate of 44 guns, and the Countess of Scarborough (Captain Piercy). The latter was a hired vessel mounting twenty 6-pounders- light guns, with few trained gunners. The advantage of the wind was with the escorting ships. They at once stretched to the southward towards an enemy of whom they had probably had warning. Jones made the signal to form line of battle, but of this Landais took no notice. He stood towards the convoy, perhaps hoping to pass by the ships of war, and to make prizes while Jones fought for his life.

It was evening, and at about six o'clock the English tacked, crossing ahead of the Americans, keeping between them and the convoy. Flamborough Head itself was by now crowded with people that the rumours of the day had drawn to the neighbourhood. Even after the sun set, a harvest moon lit the scene for their benefit. At half-past seven the first shots were exchanged between the Serapis and the Bonhomme Richard, while the Pallas was engaged with the Countess of Scarborough. The less important part of the battle was soon decided. The Pallas, more powerfully armed, found herself well able to deal with her opponent, which she took prize after the Englishman had made a creditable resistance. Unfortunately for Jones, she spent the rest of the night securing her capture, and her captain made no attempt to go to the help of his commodore.

The Alliance, a powerful ship which could have rendered Jones's victory swift and overwhelming, gave up her pursuit of the convoy soon after dark, contenting herself with circling round the Pallas and the Countess of Scarborough, firing indiscriminately at both. In the struggle between Jones and Pearson, the advantage should clearly have been with the

Englishman. Not only was his ship new, his armament considerable, his crew well trained, but the Serapis was a good sailor. Moreover, within a few minutes of opening fire, two of Jones's guns burst, killing and wounding a number of men, and damaging the deck above them. After an hour's fighting, Jones knew that his only chance of success was to grapple his opponent. It should have been Pearson's particular care to prevent this, for his advantage was in mobility and ordnance, not in point of numbers. It is a matter of debate how Jones caught the Serapis, but the details themselves are clear.

The Serapis''s jibboom caught in the starboard mizzen rigging of the Bonhomme Richard. Jones lashed it to the mizzen-mast with his own hands. The Serapis's starboard anchor then hooked her opponent's quarter, and the ships swung together bow and stern, their starboard sides touching. In close fighting there was little to choose between the opponents, but their distribution of strength became important. The lower deck battery of the Serapis with its 18-pounders smashed the Bonhomme Richard's hull into fragments and silenced her main deck ordnance, but the gun crews, driven above, reinforced the fighting tops, swept the quarter deck and forecastle of the Englishman with musketry and grenades, and forced her men below.

At this critical stage the Alliance which, had she been even tolerably handled, could have raked the Serapis and settled the issue within a few minutes, repeated her earlier manoeuvre of circling the combatants, firing at both, and doing more harm - or so Jones said later - to friend than foe. Even so, her mere presence had a dispiriting effect on Pearson and his men. The English captain was even more discomforted by a display of individual daring worthy of Jones himself. One of the Bonhomme Richard's crew crawled out on to a mainyard, carrying a bucket-full of hand-grenades. He succeeded in throwing one down the main hatchway of the Serapis, where a number of cartridges had been placed so as to be handy for the guns. The grenade fell among these.

The explosions spread the length of the ship, disabled many of the guns, and killed, wounded or scorched every man serving them. The effect was so severe that it seemed likely that the ship would have to surrender there and then. Actually, matters were nearly as bad on board the American. The carpenter reported to Jones that there was so much damage below that the ship was in danger of sinking. Hearing this, the gunner ran aft, without orders, to haul down the flag, but finding that the staff had been shot away, he began to bellow, 'Quarter! For God's sake, quarter!', until Jones stove his skull in with the butt end of a pistol.

Shortly after this incident, both captains attempted to board. Although neither was successful, the next event might have given the day to the Serapis. In the hold of the Bonhomme Richard were about a hundred prisoners taken from prizes. Shortly after the carpenter cried for quarter, the American master-at-arms went below to release them. Over a hundred men rushed on deck, and had they been organized they should have been able, with the help of their friends in the Serapis, to overwhelm their captors. But they were confused, panic-stricken, half stunned with noise, in a condition to be ordered about, but not to take the initiative. Jones, with sublime presence of mind, instantly set them to work in parties at the pumps. There they stayed, like obedient sheep.

Only one man kept enough self-possession to make his way over to the Serapis, and to tell Captain Pearson the true state of the Bo7ihomme Richard. This act of initiative was too late to be of any use. Both ships were beaten, and it was almost a matter of chance which would give in first. The matter was decided by the near presence of the Alliance, and by the fact of the Pallas's success becoming known to the English. At half past ten the Serapis struck, Jones at once taking possession. The Bonhomme Richard was with difficulty kept afloat during the night, and she sank about ten o'clock on the morning of the 26th. The state of the men was much the same as that of the ships: they were completely knocked up. The exact number of killed and wounded is uncertain but in proportion to those engaged it was the bloodiest combat of its time.

Flamborough Head was the greatest scene of Paul Jones's life. He managed to get his prizes to the Texel and later to France, where he received great honour. The King gave him a gold-hilted sword inscribed: vindicati MARIS LUDOVICUS XVI REMUNERATOR STRENUO VINDICI ('Louis XVI recognizes the services of the brave maintainer of the privileges of the sea'). His own authorities awarded him a gold medal, and he is honoured as one of the founders of the American navy, though he held no further active command. The fate of the captains of the Serapis and the Countess of Scarborough is of some interest. They were tried by court martial at Sheerness on 10 March 1780, and were honourably acquitted.

The Court held that 'Captains Pearson and Piercy, assisted by their officers and men, had not only acquitted themselves of their duty to the country, but had, in the execution of such duty, done infinite credit to themselves by a very obstinate defence against a very superior force'. The merchants of London, whose cargoes Pearson and Piercy had safeguarded, presented Pearson with a sword of honour. King George HI, with what may appear to have been some excess of enthusiasm, actually knighted him. Pearson indeed had done his best, but in the circumstances, it was far from good enough. He should have taken one of the various chances open to him to defeat his indifferently equipped though determined and skilful enemy, whose conduct of the engagement was in fact beyond praise.

Above all, he should have kept his distance, and pounded the American to pieces. Paul Jones deserves the last word about the occasion. When he heard how his antagonist had been rewarded, he remarked: 'Should I have the good fortune to fall in with him again, I'll make him a lord! ' The oddest fact of all was the continuous assertion by Landais that it was he who had defeated the Serapis. He lived years after the battle, chiefly in America, and long before his death he had utterly convinced himself of the truth of his own story.

The Naval Battle of Flamborough Head, fought on September 23, 1779, during the American Revolutionary War, had significant aftermath and outcomes that extended well beyond the immediate tactical victory. This engagement, though relatively small in scale, had considerable strategic and economic implications for both the American and British forces involved. In the short term, the battle, led by the renowned American naval commander John Paul Jones on the Bonhomme Richard, demonstrated the capability of the fledgling American navy to challenge British naval supremacy. The victory was a significant morale booster for the American cause, showcasing their resilience and determination against a formidable British fleet. For the British, the defeat was a shock, as it occurred close to their home waters, challenging the long-held perception of British naval invincibility.

This battle highlighted the vulnerability of British merchant shipping and naval dominance, especially in the North Sea and the English Channel. Economically, the battle had implications for both sides. For the Americans, the victory, albeit costly, was a symbol of their growing naval prowess and helped to bolster French support, which was crucial in terms of financial aid and military assistance. The capture of British merchant vessels also provided a much-needed economic boost through the acquisition of valuable cargoes. For the British, the defeat at Flamborough Head had economic repercussions, particularly in terms of increased insurance rates for merchant shipping and the need to divert naval resources to protect trade routes. This diversion of resources and the increased caution in merchant shipping routes had a ripple effect on British trade and economy during a time when Britain was already financially strained by the ongoing war.

In terms of military history, the Battle of Flamborough Head is often remembered for its symbolic significance rather than its tactical importance. It showcased the effectiveness of daring and unconventional tactics employed by commanders like John Paul Jones and underscored the potential of the American navy. The battle also highlighted the strategic importance of protecting merchant shipping during wartime, a lesson that would be echoed in future naval conflicts. Overall, the Battle of Flamborough Head imposed limitations on British maritime operations in home waters and provided the American forces with a significant psychological and strategic advantage. The battle remains a celebrated event in American naval history, symbolizing the audacity and skill of the American naval forces during the Revolutionary War. The great naval hero of the American War of Independence triumphed in one of the most extraordinary sea battles in history, against the British frigate 'Serapis'

6. Gibraltar and Malaga, 1704 (10th place)

In Marlborough's campaigns against the French, The Capture of Gibraltar was a result of both naval and military action, as the men managed to capture the Rock. Since they were marines, it is fitting that the British Corps of Royal Marines, who hold the highest distinction in the world, continue to wear a globe with a laurel wreath around it as their emblem. Their valour in war, "Gibraltar," is a symbol of their accomplishments both then and now, around the world. The event itself was essentially fortuitous and had nothing to do with the London government's preparations; it happened in 1704, the same year as the huge land victory at Blenheim. The greatest credit should have gone to Sir George Rooke, the admiral who had gained experience in the previous century's conflicts and knew how to turn backup plans around when the original didn't work out.

The main goals of the 1702–1703 Spanish Succession War were to determine whether Philip of France, the Spanish king Charles II, had left Spain and its dominions and should own them, and whether the powerful France of Louis XIV and his grandson's Spain should be unified. It was quite intricate and lasted for more than ten years. From Britain's perspective, the battle saw her ships fighting alongside the Dutch, longtime rivals. Additionally, the Allied fleet utilised Portugal's bases and harbours, which would prove to be extremely valuable both now and in the future. There were two setbacks in the maritime conflict. While pursuing an enemy squadron off the coast of Spanish America, Admiral Benbow was abandoned by his commanders, two of whom were eventually hanged for cowardice.

Rooke was unable to capture Cadíz in Spain. However, he discovered on the way home that a Spanish treasure fleet had entered Vigo Bay, under the protection of a French garrison. With guns from both the sea and the land covering it, the French admiral placed a boom across the inner harbour. After receiving the command to break the boom, Rooke's ships pursued Sir John Hopson and launched an assault on the treasure ships. Everything went smoothly. Even now, excellent silver coins featuring Queen Anne's picture and the word "Vigo" beneath her bust can still be recovered, despite the fact that much of the treasure was seized. The coins came from Rooke's haul. A few years later, Marlborough gave his consent for an allied assault on the renowned French port of Toulon.

The French gained strength from the arrival of a potent French fleet from Brest, and it was just as unsuccessful as the raid on Barcelona, forcing Rooke to retreat to the Atlantic. Ships commanded by Sir Clowdesley Shovell joined him off the coast of southwest Spain. Rooke and Shovell made the decision to try Ciibraltar because they didn't want to go home empty-handed. The navy swung southward. Gibraltar, the massive rock stronghold, holds a significant position in terms of geography. It appears to thrust a sword into the sea at the

Mediterranean's entry, which is open to the east. The Bay of Algeciras is seen from the western side of the rock. A narrow strip of land connects it to the nation to the north, where it appears to belong organically. Known as one of the Pillars of Hercules, along with Mount Abyla on the African side of the Straits, Gibraltar was named Mons Calpe by the Romans.

The Moorish invaders of North Africa crossed the sea and overran it in the seventh century. Tarik-ibn-Zeyad captured it, and the general's name is forever associated with it because Gibraltar is actually named Gebel Tarik, or "the Mountain of Tarik." It took Tarik fourteen years to build a palace and a citadel, and the Moors had complete control over it until the first of numerous known sieges occurred there in 1309. Ultimately, Alonzo DC Guzman's Spanish team was in charge. However, the Spanish did not regard it, and soon afterward, it turned into a haven for criminals. After the Moors left and returned, there were several sieges and conflicts over ownership until, in the end, Spanish power took control of the region in 1462. Men who swore loyalty to the Duke of Medina Sidonia, the ancestor of the commander of the Armada in 1588, garrisoned it.

The stronghold of Gibraltar, which was naturally strong, was in a vulnerable position when Rooke made the decision to invade. Although there were fortifications, primarily constructed by Emperor Charles V, father of Philip II of Spain and Don John of Austria, and a mole where the modern harbour is now located on the Algeciras side, the troops were not prepared for an attack, and the governor signed articles of surrender after nearly token resistance. Sir John Leake, commander of the Prince George, a vessel named for Queen Anne's spouse, was one of Rooke's captains. Leake bequeathed a notebook in which he detailed the short account of Rooke's triumph, showing a fine disdain for proper syntax and writing.

When the fleet was outside the port early on Sunday, July 23, 1704, the battle broke out. Leake said that around five o'clock, "the ships assigned to cannonade the town began to fire, as likewise the Bomb Vessells began to heave in their bombs." These "bombs," which were launched from near inshore and resembled mortar rounds, after roughly four hours, the firing slowed down. The ships did not have enough powder and shot to last them. When it became evident that the Spaniards had been "beaten from their guns" by eleven o'clock, those closest to the mole gave the signal for the boats to enter.

Though they had not advanced much, some had already touched down on the western side. Just after lunchtime, serious business resumed. Following further setbacks, reinforcements arrived: "the rest of the boats getting ashore under the command of Capt. Edward Whitaker, the men rallied again and got into the fort, set up a union flag, and marched to another small fort nearer the town, which was deserted by the Spaniards." Leake wrote, "Several of our boat crews having gotten ashore upon the new Mould (Mole) to take possession of the Fort, the Magezen of powder blew up, destroyed several men, and wounded Capt. Hicks who had Having had enough, the garrison summoned the town from the north gate, where the Marines were encamped, and shortly after the Admiral did the same from the south gate, where the Seamen were, and received an answer from the Governor.

The Prince of Hesse, in charge of the Dutch and German troops, also participated in the operation. The governor declared that they would surrender at eight the following day, provided that the hostages were immediately exchanged.

After doing this, Leake was able to wrap up his account by noting that the Marines arrived and took custody of the objects at four on Monday. .... If capturing Gibraltar had been simple, the battle that followed would have been more fierce. The French and Spanish responded quickly, but it appears that they were unaware of the fortress's significant worth to its adversaries. The honour of Spain was offended, and Gibraltar may become a persistent source of pain if the Dutch, Germans, and English are permitted to continue consolidating their gains. The first step in retaking it was to destroy Rooke's fleet. After being forced out of Toulon once, Rooke ought to be permanently banished from the Mediterranean.

As Rooke found, Gibraltar was most readily defended from the north, so the Spaniards launched an attack from that direction. They also quickly received Louis XIV's fleet's assistance when they requested it. The fleets met on August 13, just weeks after Rooke's victory, above Malaga, a little distance into the Mediterranean. He gave the order to his natural son, the Comte de Toulouse, to destroy the Anglo-Dutch. The combat turned out to be one of those tense, disappointing clashes typical of naval warfare. Both commanders manoeuvred inflexibly, failing to find a means to breach the enemy defence and ultimately arrive at a conclusion. Leading the van Rooke was Shovell, with Kallenberg leading the Dutch in the back.

The French, with their newly acquired fleet, ought to have made their advantage known, but the fighting was fierce and there were many casualties. Although they had the advantage of Leake, who fought in Shovell's squadron, saying that on August 14, we lay expecting them but in fact in a shattered condition, and several of our Fleet without ammunition, I believe they had enough because they sailed in a windward direction, and to keep at a distance till the 16th at night, they gave us the slip and went eastward. Nevertheless, they fought at too defensive a stance in the centre of the Allied line, and four ships had to be towed away.

There were at least fifty ships on the Anglo-Dutch line. In addition to bringing twenty-five French and Spanish galleys, the French had one more. With a history dating back to classical times, it was nearly the last time that oared men-of-war participated in a general engagement. They turned out to be ineffective. Given that propaganda is not a recent endeavour, both sides publicly declared their victories — the French and the Spanish in particular. Thirty-six enemy ships, including the admiral Rooke and the flagships of England and Holland, had allegedly been taken prisoner, and sixteen had been sunk, according to a writer in Seville. This was large-scale lying. Velez Malaga ranks as a major sea battle for good reason.

The account acknowledged the loss of four ships, "two galleys of Spain and two of France," and came to the conclusion that "the end of the remainder of the enemy is to be expected momentarily, the Comte de Toulouse having sent a squadron to the Straits of Gibraltar, that none of the enemy may escape." It was inconclusive in and of itself; neither side lost any ships; yet, Rooke could and did declare victory because all he had to do was maintain his fleet operational and close to Gibraltar in order to guarantee the Allies' capture. Nevertheless, Gibraltar remained in jeopardy.

Due to its modest size, the garrison relied on the navy, which was in dire need of resupply, for both food and munitions. Rooke would eventually have to refit, but Toulouse lost his squadron after he withdrew, sending only 10 ships to aid in the land battle. "With this reverse," a French naval officer claimed, "a regrettable reaction against the navy began in all of France." .... The army, being closer to the people, enjoyed the nation's favour and sympathy the most. Rooke's efforts went unappreciated in London, as he was replaced and Queen Anne's successor, the first of four Georges of Hanover, placed such a low value on his capture that he later offered to give it up. People and the government have shown greater common sense.

Retaining Gibraltar proved to be beneficial only four years after its conquest, as it acted as a springboard for the conquest of Minorca, the easternmost of the Balearic Islands. The island's resources were so important that the British kept possession of them for most of the eighteenth century, and there was a beautiful natural seaport at Port Mahon. Gibraltar's best hour came later, when, during the years 1780–83, it withstood its harshest siege, the governor being George Eliot, Lord Heathfield, one of the most determined officers ever deployed to the Mediterranean. But without supplies supplied to him from England under the main fleet's cover, even Heathfield would not have been able to hold out. Three main reliefs were seen.

First, in 1780, Admiral Rodney commanded a moonlight battle against Admiral de Langara in the latitude of Cape St. Vincent, which resulted in the capture of a lucrative Spanish convoy off Cape Finisterre and the capture of six ships, including the enemy flagship. The second, under Admiral Darby's command, was less dramatic overall, but Pierre-Andre Suffren's squadron was able to leave Brest for the Indian Ocean because of the lax surveillance on France. After the ships delivered their supplies, Lord Howe led the third and final expedition against a stronger enemy fleet. According to many, Howe's operation was the most challenging and fruitful he had ever performed. An important early conflict in the War of the Spanish Succession, the Naval Battle of Gibraltar in 1702, had far-reaching effects that influenced the political and economic environments of the early eighteenth century.

This battle, fought on August 24, 1702, saw Admiral George Rooke's Anglo-Dutch navy attack and seize a Spanish treasure fleet near Gibraltar. This interaction has far-reaching effects on all parties concerned. Particularly for England and the Dutch Republic, the victory gave the Grand Alliance a significant short-term boost in morale and prestige. Funding the continued war efforts against France and Spain depended heavily on the substantial cash windfall that came from the capture of the Spanish treasure ships. The Allies gained a vital naval base and control over access to the Mediterranean by seizing Gibraltar, a strategically significant location at the mouth of the Mediterranean that allowed them to impede French and Spanish maritime activity. It was a huge blow for both Spain and its ally, France. The treasure fleet's loss dealt them a serious financial blow by denying them access to vital funds for their war endeavours.

A source of national shame, the seizure of Gibraltar, a region under Spanish rule for centuries, has long-term geopolitical ramifications. The fall of Gibraltar would cause Spain and Britain to harbour ongoing animosity that went far beyond the Spanish Succession War. From the perspective of military history, the Battle of Gibraltar in 1702 demonstrated how crucial naval might is to deciding the course of larger geopolitical wars. It emphasised how important it is strategically to hold key maritime chokepoints like Gibraltar. The conflict also established a standard for coalition warfare by showcasing the potency of coordinated Anglo-Dutch naval operations. Overall, the Battle of Gibraltar gave the Grand Alliance—especially Britain—strategic and financial advantages while severely restricting the Franco-Spanish alliance's naval power and financial resources. One long-lasting consequence of the fight was the British conquest and subsequent occupation of Gibraltar, which remained a strategically significant and divisive issue in European politics for generations to come. As a result, the fight and its aftermath are considered a turning point in the military history of the early eighteenth century, influencing both the direction of the War of the Spanish Succession and the distribution of power in Europe. Under Sir George Rooke, a combined British and Dutch navy forced the Spanish Governor to give over the Rock.

7. The Four Days Battle, 1666 (9th place)

Perhaps it was inevitable that the Dutch and English would engage in naval warfare throughout the seventeenth century. Despite the fact that both countries were small, vibrant, Protestant, nautical, and united against Spain, they were physically close to one another, shared a common purpose of boosting trade abroad, and produced a resilient breed of seafarers, many of whom quickly gained combat experience. When Oliver Cromwell ruled England in the years 1652–1654, the first of several Anglo-Dutch naval conflicts occurred. With Charles II at the throne, the two navies clashed once more, a little over a decade later.

The main admirals, George Monck, Duke of Albemarle, on the English side, and de Ruyter on the Dutch side, were roughly equal in skill during the Four-Days' Battle, which took place primarily in Channel waters between June 1 and 4, 1666. According to an earlier treaty, Louis XIV had promised the Dutch that France would assist them. The London Government divided the Fleet, sending Prince Rupert down the Channel with a squadron of twenty-four ships to intercept a force that was mistakenly thought to be headed to reinforce de Ruyter. "At Whitehall, Thomas Clifford wrote to Lord

Arlington, 'There is nothing but complaints from the seamen concerning the division of the Fleet and the departure of Prince Rupert."

The sailors deserved it, as Charles II was taking a significant risk in defying the concept of focus. That defeat might have meant catastrophe if the English admirals had been inferior men. The man who would bear the weight, George Monck, was nearly sixty years old at the time and had served mostly as a professional soldier. Along with serving Charles I in England and Ireland, he had fought alongside the Dutch against Spain and was one of the main 'Generals at Sea' in the first maritime battle following the King's death. Following Oliver Cromwell's demise, he played a pivotal role in the restoration of the monarchy.

Charles was happy to discover that he was eager to return to sea duty, serving with his childhood comrade, Prince Rupert. Ever since Marten Tromp's death off Scheveningen during the Cromwellian war—during which he had also faced Monck—De Ruyter had been the premier leader of the Netherlands. He was about the same age as his opponent, had nearly the same amount of life experience, and was simply better as a maritime commander. His compatriot Obdam had suffered a reverse at the hands of the Duke of York the previous year, and he was eager to exact revenge. He had just returned from an expedition against English colonies and factories on the Guinea Coast.

He had a great chance when the English fleet split up since he had 90 ships to fight against only 50, and he never shied away from a fight. With a fair easterly breeze that later shifted to the south-west and heavy weather, the Dutch set off for the English coast. De Ruyter stopped between Dunkirk and the

Downs to prevent being forced back. Monck saw them from a windward position, and he chose to assault despite his recognised numerical disadvantage. The day following the battle, a narrative from Monck's flagship, the Royal Charles, states, 'The General called immediately a Council of Flag Officers, which being done, the sign was put out to fall into the line of battle.' These words are significant because they signalled Monck's intention to form a line quickly and attack as a unified body before de Ruyter could get his ships into order. It was the most audacious move ever, and in the case of a weaker foe, it could have resulted in the Dutch being dispersed or even in an incredible win over overwhelming odd.

Things went smoothly for the English at first. Monck threw his entire force at Marten's son, Cornelis Tromp's squadron, which was in the Dutch fleet's van. At that point, the sea was so high that Monck was unable to deploy his lower tiers of cannons, so Tromp severed his cables, setting off an English and Dutch running battle for the French coast. De Ruyter also severed his cords with his main body, moving in tandem with Tromp. Being too leeward, he was unable to stop the loss of one of his larger ships and would need some time to intervene, unless at a great distance. Monck moved about when he approached Dunkirk, where the coast was shelved, and on his way back, he was rudely handled by ships that had not previously engaged.

Two English flagships, Berkeley's and Harman's, were cut off". Their fates were very different. Sir Wlliam Berkeley in the Swiftsure, a young man of twenty-seven, with a ship which had been launched eighteen years before he was born, was boarded on both sides. He would accept no quarter, and at last, being wounded in the throat by a musket ball, he retired to his cabin, where he was found dying, stretched out upon a table almost covered with his own blood. The ship surrendered. In Harman's case, the Henry, which was even older than the Swiftsure, was grappled by a fire-ship. By heroic exertions a lieutenant managed to cast off the grappling irons. Then a second fire-ship, approaching on the other side, set the sails alight, an incident which so terrified the crew that a number jumped overboard.

Harman ran among the rest with his sword drawn, forcing them to get the fire under control. Then one of the top-sail yards fell from aloft, pinned Harman to the deck, and broke his leg. Soon afterwards, a third fire-ship tried to grapple, but she was sunk by the Henrys broadside before she could achieve her aim. At this stage Evertzoon, the Dutch second-in-command, bore down and offered Harman quarter. The reply came swiftly: 'No, no, it is not come to that yet!', and Harman, with another broadside, drove the Dutch tt) a respectful distance, saving his ship. Monck's bold opening had failed, chiefly because of the difficulty his ships met with in keeping together, which was due in part to stress of weather. Yet for a commander inferior in strength, he had not done badly. He had lost one flagship, and many other ships had suffered damage and he had inflicted loss.

More than one Dutch ship had' become forced to return home, two had been sunk outright while the moral effect of his tactics was immense 'Nothing equals the beautiful order of the! English at sea ' wrote a French observer in de Ruyter's fleet, they bring all their fire to bear upon those who draw near them' - mutual support was the paramount virtue of a 'line' in battle. 'They fight like cavalry which is handled according to rule . . . whereas the Dutch advance like cavalry whose squadrons leave their ranks and come separately to the charge.' Night ended the first phase of the encounter, Monck and knew that his sternest test would come next day

Once again, he decided that the best form of defence was attack. We engaged again about 7 of the clocks,' said the writer from the Royal Charles and our General did all that man could do, both by his conduct and valour in exposing himself to obtain a victory: but seeing man of ours gone away, and those that were left much torn he prudently resolved to make a retreat.' In his attack, Monck once again had Cornelis Tromp at a disadvantage, and might have captured him but for Michiel de Ruyter move in hauling up to his rescue.

Shortly; Afterwards, Tromp went on board de Ruyter's flagship his seamen cheered, but de Ruyter said gravely' This is no time for rejoicing, but rather for tears.' What he meant was that he had been forced to alter his dispositions to come to Tromp's aid, that his squadrons were disordered, and that the English, had they not been crippled, might have pressed their advantage. But Monck was in a bad state, and although his rearmost ship was able to damage the Dutch commander-in chief to such a degree that she had, for a time, to withdraw, his own immediate object was to retire in good order, shepherding his most damaged ships, and showing a brave front with the rest. Fighting became intermittent, the English slowly retreating towards their own coast.

Next day this retreat continued, Monck giving orders to burn three disabled ships. Unfortunately, one of the finest ships in the English fleet, the Royal Prince, ran ashore on the Galloper Sand, and was captured by Tromp, though Monck's line was so steady that he was otherwise unmolested. Sir George Ayscue's surrender affected him only personally, for to Tromp's disgust the Prince had to be burnt to prevent her recapture, and it was the admiral alone who was borne off to Holland. At one time Monck's own flagship went aground, and there was a danger that she might share the fate of Ayscue's. John Sheffield, a young man who was later to become a duke and a notable patron of men of letters, was serving in the Royal Charles as a volunteer. He recalled later that, before the ship had been got off, he 'spied the General charging a little pistol and putting it in his pocket'. As Monck had been heard to say that he would never allow himself to be taken prisoner, the pistol was obviously intended to blow up the magazine as a last resource: 'and therefore,' said Sheffield, 'Mr Savill and I in a laughing way most mutinously resolved to throw him overboard in case we should ever catch him going down to the powder room.' If one thing more than another could have been calculated to put Prince Rupert into a frenzy, it would have been the thought of taking his twenty-four ships on a wild goose chase, leaving his fellow commander-in-chief, for whom he felt affection and respect, to fight it out at a disadvantage with the Dutch admiral.

In point of fact, as soon as it was known that Monck was likely to become engaged, the Admiralty signed an order for Rupert's recall and sent it to Arlington, expecting that he would at once countersign and despatch it. But Arlington happened to be in bed, and nobody dared wake him, so the order never went. Fortunately, the sound of distant firing reached Rupert's squadron. Guessing what had happened, he reversed course on his own responsibility and made his way back at his best speed to join his colleague. The swaying struggle in which Monck and de Ruyter had been engaged since June, over a wide expanse of sea, gave Rupert just the necessary time to make the junction, and it was not a moment too soon. 'About one o'clock Sunday (3 June) in the afternoon we discovered the Prince's squadron standing with us,' reported the observer in the Royal Charles. ' The shouts of joy that went from our ships at the sight so disordered the Dutch, that those ships of theirs that were almost come within shot of us, shortened sail and fell back again into the main body of their Fleet.'

Prince Rupert, as he arrived at the scene of action, must have seen in a moment how hard Monck was pressed. Ayscue had just surrendered, the Dutch had the advantage of the wind, and their numbers were at last beginning to tell. Soon after nightfall on 3 June, the English joint commanders were able to confer, and to decide how to conduct the final phase of the action. It could scarcely last much longer. The crews were nearing exhaustion; powder and shot were beginning to run low and, on both sides, ships were being forced in increasing numbers to return to port for repair. With two men of the calibre of Monck and Rupert, it was almost inevitable that the decision should be to continue to attack, in the hope of wearing down the enemy by continual melees.

If Monck's ships were battered, Rupert's were fresh, and as always, the Prince was eager for a fight. Five times, during the course of the last day, English and Dutch engaged in close action. Rupert had his fill. His flagship, the Royal James, was soon in the thick of it, losing her main yard and main top, and by the evening the Royal Charles was so damaged aloft that ' neither the Prince nor the General could work their ships, or lead on the Fleet'. Dc Ruyter had also had enough. 'In the night,' said the observer in the Royal Charles, 'we mended our rigging, but the General's squadron having spent almost all their powder and shot it was impossible to engage again. The Dutch left us in the night, being as unfit to fight as we, and their loss doubtless at least as great as ours.'

So ended the Four-Days' Battle, with great damage to both sides, but greater to the English, who had one flag officer killed in action, another taken prisoner, and a third, Sir Christopher Myngs, mortally wounded. Myngs who was in the van of the English fleet in the last fighting, was the subject of a touching incident, recorded by Samuel Pepys from direct observation. Myng's body was brought home, and he was buried in London. Pepys was there, in an Admiralty coach, when about a dozen able, lusty proper men came to the coach side with tears in their eyes, and one of them spoke for the rest . . . 'We are here a dozen of us that have long known and served our dead commander . . . and have now done the last office of laying him in the ground.

We would be glad we had any other to offer after him, and in revenge of him. All we have is our lives; if you will please to get His Royal Highness to give us a fire-ship among us all, here is a dozen of us, out of all which choose you one to be commander, and the rest of us, whoever he is, will serve him; and if possible, do that shall show our memory of the dead commander, and our revenge!' Such were the heights of devotion in the fleet after this extraordinary battle, without doubt a defeat for the English, but a costly triumph for their opponents. Monck and Rupert lost five thousand killed, three thousand prisoners and seventeen ships, eight sunk and nine in Dutch hands.

Yet within seven weeks they were ready for sea again, and on St James's Day, 25 July, off Orfordness, they had their revenge, causing de Ruyter the loss of twenty ships for a single ship of their own. Following up the victory, Sir Robert Holmes destroyed a hundred and fifty ships in the line, and burnt the storehouses of Brandaris. Splendid as the feat was, it did not altogether satisfy Rupert. After the St James's Day battle, he wrote a brief despatch to his cousin the Duke of York in which the sentence occurred: ' I hope your Highness will be satisfied with our endeavours, though some gross errors have been committed by Persons, not in point of courage but want of conduct.' By 'conduct' Rupert meant strict obedience to the Admiral, a characteristic which, as signals and instructions grew more precise, would be looked for as much as valour in the sea officers of the future.

The war was not to end happily for England, since Charles II made a second blunder. Shortly after the July victory, he laid up the fleet. In June the following year the Dutch sailed up the Medway, captured the Royal Charles, and threw all London into a panic. Pepys heard of English voices calling from Dutch ships: ' We did heretofore fight for tickets: now we fight for dollars! ' It was an ignominious moment, the result of throwing away, by short-sighted ineptitude, what had been gained by resolution. Once more it was de Ruyter, with a cruising force, who ensured the success of the operation, enabling him to end the war in a blaze of glory.

The same French observer in his flagship, the Comte de Guichc, who had seen with what discipline Monck ordered his fleet, gave posterity the best thumb-nail sketch of de Ruyter during the time of the Four-Days' Battle. It was one which may serve to typify his character throughout a long and illustrious career. ' I never saw him other than even-tempered,' he said, 'and when victory was assured, saying always that it was the good God that gives it to us. Amid the disorders of the Fleet and the appearance of loss, he seemed only to be moved by the misfortune to his country, but always submissive to the Will of God. He had something of the frankness and lack of polish of our patriarchs, and to conclude what I have to say of him, I will relate that the day after the victory I found him sweeping his own cabin and feeding his chickens.'

The Naval Battle of the Four Days, fought from June 11 to June 14, 1666, between the English and Dutch fleets, stands as a pivotal moment in naval history, with far-reaching aftermath and outcomes that shaped the strategic and economic landscapes of the belligerents. In the immediate aftermath, the Dutch, under the command of Admiral Michael de Ruyter, emerged with a tactical advantage. The English fleet, led by Prince Rupert of the Rhine and George Monck, Duke of Albemarle, suffered significant losses, both in terms of ships and manpower. This victory bolstered the morale of the Dutch and solidified de Ruyter's reputation as a formidable naval commander.

Strategically, the battle had profound implications. In the short term, it disrupted English naval dominance and challenged their control over the seas. The English Navy, facing a shortage of supplies and manpower, found itself stretched thin, struggling to maintain its extensive maritime commitments. This setback in naval power temporarily weakened England's ability to protect its merchant fleets, which had significant economic repercussions. The loss of ships and the cost of rebuilding the fleet strained England's finances, already burdened by the ongoing Second Anglo-Dutch War.

For the Dutch, the victory in the Four Days Battle had immediate economic benefits. It allowed for the safer passage of Dutch merchant ships, which was crucial for the Netherlands, a nation heavily reliant on maritime trade. The victory also enhanced Dutch bargaining power in international affairs and boosted national pride. In the long term, the battle underscored the importance of naval power in determining the outcome of conflicts. It highlighted the need for sustainable naval logistics and strategic planning.

For England, the defeat was a wake-up call, leading to reforms in naval administration and shipbuilding, which would eventually contribute to its emergence as a dominant naval power in the following centuries. The Four Days Battle, thus, had a lasting impact on both England and the Netherlands. It altered the course of the Second Anglo-Dutch War and played a crucial role in shaping the future of naval warfare. The limitations it imposed on the English Navy and the advantages it conferred upon the Dutch fleet marked a significant shift in the balance of naval power in the 17th century, with enduring effects on the military, economic, and political landscapes of Europe.

8. The Nile, 1798. (8th Place)

John Jervis, Earl St. Vincent, was one of Howe's closest friends, and St. Vincent's most famous student was Horatio Nelson. Hawke had served under Howe, and Hawke had served under Anson; Anson had recollections of commanders who had participated in the final battles against the Dutch. There was no break in the line of naval tradition since the first time he went to sea at the age of twelve. Nelson had a singular goal in mind: using her fleet to elevate his nation. He had fought alongside Hughes against Hyder Ali in the East Indies as a young man, having been born in 1758. He had fought on land and at sea: on land, against the French in Corsica, where he had lost his sight in his right eye, and against the Spanish and French in the Atlantic and Mediterranean in the West Indies and North America, where he had lost his right arm in an attempt on Tenerife. His first significant opportunity occurred while he was a commodore, at the battle of Cape St. Vincent.

It was 1797, and Jervis had gained an earldom from it. Nelson had stepped outside the designated line, acting independently and securing the capitulation of two vessels.

His commander-in-chief was unlikely to forget the incident, and when Nelson recovered from his wounds and rejoined the fleet as a rear admiral in the spring of 1798, Jervis provided him with a rare opportunity for distinction and the tools to achieve it. The hardships of the present seemed to Great Britain no different from those of the American Revolutionary War. On land, the French were unstoppable because they had found a prodigy with incredible skill and ambition in Napoleon Bonaparte.

Despite the fact that Jervis's navy had to evacuate the Mediterranean, his victory in battle had only temporary benefits. When word spread that Channel and later Spithead ships were mutinying, they were lost in the terror that flooded every heart. To top it all off, it was evident by the first few months of 1798 that the French were organising a very significant and covert project. After touring the coasts of Flanders and Northern France, Napoleon reported to Paris that "we shall not gain naval supremacy for some years." The most audacious and challenging mission ever attempted was to invade England without that supremacy.

To put it in the vernacular of the day, we need to "shake England to her marrow-bones." After weighing the pros and cons, Napoleon finally said that "an Eastern expedition would menace Britain's trade with the Indies." France remained hopeful about achieving greatness in India. Not only would Napoleon bring them back to life, but he would also make them a reality. Not only was an Eastern expedition feasible, but it was also very desirable, and there was no obstacle to it, barring the British from making a strong comeback to the Mediterranean. Every significant port on the French and Italian Riviera was working towards a project whose goal was only known to a select few within weeks of the decision. For various reasons, both sides hurried.

After spending just two days with St. Vincent, Nelson set off on a mission to learn more about the events in the Mediterranean and, if feasible, to overthrow the French fleet before it could serve its intended purpose. On May 8, Nelson crossed the Straits of Gibraltar in three-line ships — two frigates and a sloop. It was the day prior to Napoleon's arrival in Toulon. In a Gulf of Lions gale less than two weeks later, the Vanguard almost sank and suffered damage to its mast.

The French had moved away with uncertainty, scattering Nelson's frigates. This is to give you permission and direction to move on with your squadron in order to locate the significant armaments using every available method. ...at Marseilles, Genoa, and Toulon,' Nelson's orders ran. Speculation pointed to Portugal or Ireland on the one hand and Sicily, Malta, and Corfu on the other. In actuality, St. Vincent had bet everything on Napoleon's being an eastern, not a western, destination by splitting and thereby weakening his fleet. Nelson would have committed an unpardonable act if he had allowed the French to cross the Straits of Gibraltar without notice.

As it is, he was forced from his station, and he had no idea that the enemy may be carrying out the same manoeuvre. Even though things appeared dire, they were not quite that bad. When the ten additional ships that would make up his full force joined him after Nelson had re-fitted the flagship at sea with the help of the other line ships, he knew that the worst had not happened. However, where was Napoleon at the time? Napoleon was in Malta.

On June 9, his massive armada made landfall on the island. The French members of the Knights of St. John had declined to serve their fellow countrymen, and the order was corrupt. The Grand Master gave up with hardly any opposition at all. In a few days, Napoleon had seized the island's riches, completely restructured its operations, stationed a force in Valetta, and continued his journey. Because Nelson's captains were all seasoned veterans, he sought advice from the senior officers when the admiral discovered he was receiving no news about the French, not even from Naples, which was typically a fount of intelligence. Troubridge of the Culloden, Sir James Saumarez of the Orion, and Darby of the Bellerophon Everyone was in agreement that Egypt was the most likely location for a French attack; therefore, Nelson rushed there. He was unable to expand his search due to the lack of frigates, and during the night, the ships passed Bonaparte's.

After pursuing the French, Nelson's fleet discovered them berthed at and near Alexandria. After failing in his pursuit of his opponent all the way through the Mediterranean, Nelson made the decision to launch an instant attack on that August day. At times, Nelson had faith in the commanders of his ships; they behaved as though the Admiral's commands were unnecessary, and they had an implicit understanding of the combat strategy and plan, much like the Agincourt heroes did. He never felt let down, even though he gave a lot and expected a lot. Nelson may be eager to launch an assault, but what about Bruery? He had enough time to secure his position. In a sandy bay, shoals of fish shielded him.

On Bequier, a small island where the French had installed a battery, one flank rested while the other rested on the mainland. The line's ships were inshore when the frigates and lighter craft arrived. If Brueys had been a self-assured man, he could have grinned at the idea of Nelson receiving such a warm reception should he dare to storm in. If they had been in his position, An enemy facing an anchored fleet that was ready for action on its own terms would have been the last thing Nelson and a dozen other British admirals could have hoped for. Ashore, Brueys hosted watering parties. He recalled them and prepared for action, though it took him an hour or two to be certain that Nelson would assault that afternoon at any rate. Nelson had the wind at his back and enough time, before nightfall, to finish a tactical masterwork.

His main strategy was so straightforward that he could sum it up to Lord Howe in less than thirty words: "I was able to throw as much fire as I pleased on a few ships by attacking the enemy's van and centre with the wind blowing directly along their line." Nelson accomplished what every admiral since the dawn of time had hoped would happen. Two errors made by his opponent worked in his favour. The van was to the west, and most of Brueys's fleet lay in a little bend, so Nelson had to sail into the harbour under heavy fire. The enemy's proximity to Bequier Island necessitated a north eastern to south-westerly onslaught.

If Brueys had deployed artillery to defend his flank with greater vigour rather than a few light pieces, the British would have undoubtedly suffered greatly. As it was, Brueys's recklessness allowed him to circumvent the head of the French line and launch an attack from the inshore area, where the enemy's guns were probably unprepared, much to the surprise and delight of Foley, the captain of the leading ship, as details of the French position became apparent. Afterwards, more captains saw that the French anchorages were not sufficiently close to one another and that some areas could allow an experienced individual to breach the formation and rake an adversary in the process. Samuel Hood, a famous admiral's kinsman, trailed behind in jealousy where Foley led.

The Audacious anchored where she could rake the Conquerant, near the stern, as all of Nelson's ships did, with a spring on the cable to facilitate movement. Theseus came next, and in the Orion, Sir James Saumarez. It was becoming late in the day when Nelson appeared in the Vanguard. Attacking the French on the seaward side, the flagship and every subsequent ship moved carefully down the line, blowing up everything in their way. Troubridge, a longtime friend of Nelson's, was the lone unfortunate captain.

Despite running the Culloden into a shoal off Bequier Island, he managed to manoeuvre the final two ships into the bay without incident. Once there, they took up their positions as flaming ships and gunflashes illuminated the calm Egyptian night. Everybody knew their role, Nelson said. With Brueys's L'Orient, her chest full of riches, in the middle of his line, it was up to the Bellerophon to assault her. "I was sure each would feel for a French ship." Twelve years old, with 74 guns, the Bellerophon had already seen a lot of rough seas. With her massive size and tens of cannons, the L'Orient was the most formidable vessel in the French fleet. Her early broadsides almost completely destroyed the British.

Captain Darby and every officer had been killed or wounded within the first hour and a half, and the Bellerophon was driven from the queue, nearly wrecked. She was saved mainly by the initiative of a volunteer, Mr. Hindmarsh, who managed somehow to hoist a scrap of sail and make off" into the darkness. Shaken as the bellerophon was, she had done her work. The L'Orient was on fire, and her teeth were so drawn that she became an easy prey for the Alexander and Swiftsure, who, one on each side, made her survival unlikely. After the Vanguard had been engaged for some time with the Spartiate, Nelson was wounded. A piece of iron hit his forehead, above his sightless eye.

He streamed with blood, and he was forced to go below, believing himself to have but a brief time to live. He refused to claim attention before the 'brave fellows' who were already in the sick berth, which was the sort of consideration that is never forgotten, but the surgeon soon reassured him that, although messy and painful, his injury was not serious. Nelson returned on deck to view the most terrible incident of a tremendous night. At about ten o'clock, it was seen that fires on the French flagship were spreading beyond control and that men had begun to throw themselves into the water. Suddenly, with a roar so shattering that every ship in the harbour believed she had herself been struck, the ship blew up.

This marked the one great, unnatural, awe-inspiring pause in the battle. After a shower of flaming debris had descended, some of it setting fire to sails in the Alexander, men sank down by their guns, exhausted. There they slept side-by-side, as it were, of their sleeping enemy', as a captain described it. When battle was resumed, only two French ships of the line and two frigates were left un-sunk, ungrounded, or untaken. They were beaten out of the bay by Rear-Admiral Pierre Villeneuve, whom Bonaparte was later to call a lucky man!

The state of Aboukir Bay as dawn broke on August 2, 1798, was one of the most extraordinary in history. 'Victory is not a name strong enough for such a scene,' said Nelson, and as usual, he was right. He had achieved his masterpiece, and in his letter to Lord Howe, he said, 'Had it pleased God that I had not been wounded and stone-blind? There cannot be a doubt but that every ship would have been in our possession.' Then, thinking that perhaps this implied a reflection on his 'Band of Brothers', he added, 'But here let it not be supposed that any officer is to blame. No; on my honour, I am satisfied each did his very best.' The 'bests' may have differed, but even the least of them was creditable by any standard. Nelson's captains had set an example for all time, and the admiral himself, in Conrad's words, had 'brought heroism into the line of duty'.

Nelson always preached completion. It was not enough to beat your foe, as Howe had done on the Glorious First of June; the matter must be pursued relentlessly, the harvest gathered in. After giving thanks to the God in whom he believed so trustingly, Nelson set about the business of exploiting his triumph. Ships were repaired, prizes made sea-worthy, dispatches written (in duplicate, a wise precaution as the originals were captured in the Leander), a blockade of the coast was organised, and an officer was sent to India to notify the East India Company of the result of the battle.

The effects of Nelson's success would undoubtedly be felt in India, and the gratitude of the directors was such that they sent Nelson a present of £10,000. Not only was the victory one in which consummate skill and judgement had been shown, but its effect upon Europe was electric. It was the first major reverse Bonaparte had suffered. The French army was cut off" in Egypt, and although, given luck, the Commander-in-Chief, by deserting his army, might escape, it would be secretly. Forever destroyed was his dream of advancing into India. "I know, my dear Sir, what joy you would feel at the unparalleled victory of Nelson," Captain Collingwood, who was in charge of HMS Excellent at the time, wrote to a relative from Portsmouth a few months after the battle. Yes, it was a charming thing.

This was the professional judgement of a brother officer: "The Frenchman found himself assailed before he had determined how best hc should repel the assault, and when victory had decided on our side, the fruits of it were carefully gathered in." It was not so much the vigour of the attack as it was the promptitude that gave him the advantage so quickly. There were other tributes that were more dramatic. For example, Lord Spencer, the leader of the Admiralty at the time, was so terrified of Nelson's exploit that he fainted. Nelson received honours and a peerage from numerous sovereigns. And much more: he won a place in the hearts of his people that he has never relinquished, even among his fellow compatriots.

The Naval Battle of the Nile, fought on August 1, 1798, was a pivotal moment in military history that had a lasting impact on the strategic and economic dynamics of the late 18th century. With Admiral Horatio Nelson leading the British Royal Navy to a resounding victory over the French fleet under François-Paul Brueys d'Aigalliers, this conflict had far-reaching implications for both France and Britain as well as the larger geopolitical picture.

The French navy in the Mediterranean suffered serious damage in the immediate aftermath. Napoleon Bonaparte's army was essentially left stuck in Egypt when the French fleet was destroyed at Aboukir Bay, cutting off their sea-based supply and escape routes. The French Army's inability to project force there due to their isolation had disastrous strategic ramifications for them and undermined Napoleon's larger objectives in the Middle East.

The British victory at the Nile was a strategic coup for them, not just a tactical one. It strengthened British naval dominance in the Mediterranean, which was important for the continuing war against Napoleonic France. From an economic standpoint, Britain's naval superiority bolstered the stability of its overseas colonies and secured important trading routes, especially to India. In addition, the victory had a profound psychological effect, elevating British pride and spirit during a period when French expansionism was a real threat.

The Battle of the Nile had a significant long-term impact on European geopolitics. The fact that Britain's victory inspired countries like Russia, the Ottoman Empire, and Austria to join the struggle against Napoleon played a significant role in the establishment of the Second Coalition against France. This alliance was vital in keeping French expansion in check and ultimately leading to Napoleon's collapse. The conflict also had a long-term effect on naval strategy and technology. Naval commanders of later generations studied and imitated Nelson's daring decision to fight the French fleet at close quarters in the middle of the night, among other creative tactics he used at the Nile. In conclusion, the Naval Battle of the Nile was a pivotal event that altered the political and economic climate of its era, in addition to being a resounding British victory. It opened the door for an era of British naval dominance that would extend well into the 19th century and placed severe restrictions on French naval and imperial ambitions.

9. Lake Erie, 1813 (7th Place)

At the westernmost point of Lake Erie, on the American side of the lake, there is a very tall monument that honours Commodore Oliver Hazard Perry. During one of the most tragic wars in history, it honours the contributions of a remarkable individual throughout the conflict. In 1812, a fight between the United States of America and Great Britain pressed itself on the wider, life-and-death struggle that Europe had been engaged in for such a long time. This conflict was brought about by a lack of patience and understanding on both sides of the conflict.

The cause was twofold: first, the disruption of American trade as a result of Britain's control on the Continent through sea blockade; second, the continual sequence of annoyances, which sometimes amounted to actual violence, as a result of British naval parties boarding American ships in their search for deserters. The United Kingdom had an insatiable need for sailors to be a part of her extensive fleet; however, there was never enough of them, and the officers who grabbed them were not always careful.

The majority of the fighting that took place during the war

took place on the Great Lakes, and more specifically on Lake Erie. This was because the United States of America regarded the conflict as an opportunity to invade Canada through the Great Lakes. Despite the fact that their waters were fresh and located inland, they were the location of operations that involved regular naval officers and substantial warships. These activities have a claim to consideration as having produced at least one significant combat

They urged the use of as much expertise, determination, and initiative as was required for everything that was taking place on the ocean at the time. The Great Lakes were rarely in a state of balance due to the opposing forces that were acting on them. First, one side triumphed over the other, and then the other side did the same. There were raids, sorties, captures of outposts, marches, and clashes on land and water, and there were always three problems that pushed both sides: a lack of troops, difficult supplies, and the requirement to not only fight but also launch ships. The vast majority of the vessels' chances of surviving the open sea were extremely low. The ship was constructed out of unseasoned lumber, and the ship that was created this year was the ship that would be built the following year.

Additionally, the ship had a shallow draft, and it was held together by wooden pegs even in places where nails would have been considered vital. It was anything that could be scraped together that served as their weaponry, and it included everything from cannonades to muskets. In the summer of 1813, Perry was successful in gaining dominance over Lake Erie. He had just moved to the neighborhood and was twenty-eight years old. He was a man of strong emotions, ardent, and active. It is not unusual for characters of this type to exhibit a certain amount of sentiment. In Captain R. H.

Barclay RX, he faced a worthy adversary who was an experienced officer who had served in the military.

Trafalgar, you are here; he lost an arm to the enemy. While Perry was in the process of launching a new ship, he became aware of the news that Sir Philip Broke had successfully captured the American frigate Chesapeake off the coast of Boston, as well as the passing of her courageous captain. The reprimand served as a source of motivation for him, and he memorialized the deceased commander by naming the new ship the Lawrence. Additionally, he commissioned the creation of a blue flag with Lawrence's instructions stitched on it: "Do not give up the ship."

If he had been a contemporary expert in propaganda, he would have branded the feeling as pessimistic or, at best, negative; yet, his own troops understood exactly what he meant. The Niagara was Perry's second ship, while the Caledonia was his third. The Caledonia was, in fact, a warship that Elliott, Perry's second in command, had stolen from the British the previous October. Considering how unconventional the construction of the larger ships on either side was, it would have been difficult for a shipwright to categorise them. In spite of the fact that there were a number of gunboats that were equipped with schooners, the huge Lawrence and Niagara represented around two-thirds of Perry's strength. Due to the fact that Perry had no prior expertise in the field of operations, it was a fortunate circumstance for him that the British gave him five weeks to prepare before the day of the combat.

It was named after a British victory early in the war, and it was the largest ship that Barclay ever built. Both the Lawrence and the Niagara rivers were equal to her in terms of size, but not in terms of strength. There was only one other significant British unit, and that was the Queen Charlotte. The smaller vessels were inferior to Perry's in terms of the amount of metal they contained. Using arithmetic, it is possible that Barclay's entire army was around two-thirds as powerful as his opponent's, or even slightly more powerful. Approximately halfway along the American side of the lake, Perry's primary centre of operations was located at Presqu'Isle. When Perry had the strength to blockade, he used an anchorage off Bass Island, in what is now known as the Put-in-Bay cluster.

This was close enough for the British to threaten them. Barclay's was located at Maiden, which was located to the west. Despite the fact that the British held control of Lake Huron and the Straits of Detroit, they were running out of supplies, including food. Furthermore, there was nothing available to them from the west, and their situation was so fragile that the only way to restore it was to regain control of Lake Erie. Barclay launched an assault on September 10th, first taking advantage of the wind's favourable presence.

This caused a shift, and Perry, who was also eager to engage, then began to close in on the military line of the British. First, Barclay had a schooner in front of him, then the Detroit, then another schooner, then the Queen Charlotte, and finally, a schooner was in the back of the pack. Since the decision on the matter would be made between these four ships, Perry's order of sailing had assigned the Lawrence to the Detroit and the Niagara to the Queen Charlotte. This was because the issue would be determined between these four ships. In the beginning, Perry's flagship was the one that absorbed the brunt of the action: it was most likely the wind that plummeted, and it was most surely the Laurence and Detroit that ended up taking the shock.

Perry looked for help, but he was unsuccessful. On the other hand, Perry and his Kentuckians were the only ones who could match the bravery of Barclay's troops, who consisted of Canadians, soldiers, and a few seamen. Barclay's crew stayed firm in their faith. These guns were considered to be of a primitive nature. Snapping pistols over loose powder that was heaped up in the touch-holes was the method that was used to fire them. In the smaller boat, the supremacy of the United States quickly became apparent; nevertheless, in one instance, a gun jumped off its carriage and disappeared into the hatchway, and another gun burst.

The Queen Charlotte, which had not been assaulted by either the Niagara or the Caledonia, pushed up the line and brought her guns to bear on the Lawrence, which was already struggling with the Detroit. This occurred during the heat of the conflict. Shortly after, Perry's flagship was destroyed by gunfire. Casualties continued to mount on both sides. When it came to the British ships, all of the captains and lieutenants were either killed or wounded, and Barclay himself was struck in five different places. Perry was able to survive, maintain his composure, and ultimately save the day for the Americans. It had been more than two hours since the action began, and he still had one boat that was unharmed. It was in this fashion that he had actually rowed to the Niagara, simulating the actions of an admiral during the old Dutch battles, and he had brought his priceless blue flag with him.

At this point, the Lawrence had stopped making noise, and the exhausted British believed that the combat had come to an end and that they had emerged victorious. Perry had a different point of view. When he arrived at Niagara, the wind picked up, and he immediately assumed leadership of the situation. He recognised the opportunity to attack with a new ship on a line that was now disorganised. As of this point, the British, who had suffered casualties among their leaders, were in trouble. Their smaller ships had dispersed to the leeward side, with the majority of them incurring damage, and the Detroit and the Queen Charlotte came into conflict with one another. The next thing the British knew, the Niagara was upon them, and Perry was raging for vengeance.

Elliott had been dispatched to rouse the smaller Americans, and their expectations were quickly exceeded. After Detroit and Queen Charlotte had been captured, the smaller vessels were progressively collected up following their capture. Detroit and Queen Charlotte had very little fight left in them. A complete and utter defeat, which had appeared to be so improbable, was staring the British in the face. Prior to the fading of dawn, the flag was brought down, and Perry triumphantly returned to the Lawrence, which had been seriously damaged. With Lake Erie secured as a result of the operation, the British force that was ashore, which was on the verge of starvation, had no choice but to retreat.

The Americans were successful in capturing the town of Detroit, which was the most significant victory for the British, and the entire United States was, for the time being, free of invaders. We have now confronted our adversary, and they are now ours. That was the summary that Perry provided of his exploit. To a certain extent, it was exclusively his own. Because he was resourceful and refused to acknowledge defeat, he had thrilled his nation, and he was deserving of the monument that bears his name. An important turning point in the War of 1812 was the Naval Battle of Lake Erie, which took place on September 10, 1813.

The battle had repercussions that extended far beyond the immediate tactical success that it brought about. This action, in which a British squadron was destroyed by a United States naval force that was still in its infancy and was commanded by Oliver Hazard Perry, had enormous ramifications not just for the United States but also for the broader economy and history. There were immediate strategic repercussions that resulted from the American victory at Lake Erie in the short term. It assured that the United States maintained control over the lake, which was an essential component in the war's northern theatre of operations.

The United States was able to strengthen their military activities in the region by employing this control, which made it easier and safer for them to transport troops and supplies between locations. The British suffered a huge setback as a result of taking the loss. The disruption of their supply lines and the weakening of their strategic position in the Great Lakes region ultimately led to their defeat in the Battle of the Thames. This was the cause of their abandonment of Detroit and Fort Malden.

A significant economic benefit accrued to the United States as a result of the victory at Lake Erie. The control of the lake made it easier for the United States to engage in commerce and transportation in the surrounding area, which was essential for the economic growth of the new nation. It also caused disruptions in commercial lines between the United Kingdom and Canada, which resulted in the application of economic pressure that would eventually lead to the negotiation of peace. The Battle of Lake Erie had significant repercussions on the naval and military growth of the United States throughout the course of a prolonged period of time. In addition to being a source of national pride, the victory contributed to the development of a sense of naval identity and capability in the United States.

It was a demonstration of the efficacy of American shipbuilding and naval strategy, which encouraged additional investments in naval forces. Throughout the course of American naval history, the battle has been revered as a seminal point in the history of the navy. The legendary declaration of American resiliency and determination that Perry made after the battle, "We have met the enemy, and they are ours," has become a symbol of the nation's tenacity and determination. Additionally, the fight had repercussions for the post-war relationship between the United States of America and Britain.

It played a role in the construction of a lasting peace and ultimately led to the establishment of a long-term boundary agreement between the United States of America and Canada. In conclusion, the Naval Battle of Lake Erie was not only a military conflict; rather, it was a turning point that transformed the strategic landscape, economic landscape, and national landscape of the United States. In addition to laying the groundwork for American territorial expansion and naval development, it imposed severe constraints on the military strategy that the British employed in North America.

10. Mobile, 1864 (6th Place)

It was fitting that Southern-born David Farragut, the most exceptional sailor to emerge from the American Civil War and commander of the Union naval forces for nearly the entirety of the conflict, would face off against Confederate commander Franklin Buchanan of the Merrimac. While Farragut is deserving of a place in any gallery of naval heroes, his life story differs significantly from that of admirals whose careers were developed in the heat of combat, as Farragut entered the service much later in life. In the year 1 801, David Farragut was born in eastern Tennessee.

His father was of Spanish origin, having left Minorca during the Revolution and having briefly been a sailing master in the navy within the military. From a very young age, Farragut served in the Pacific as well as most other parts of the world. There, an English frigate with significantly more firepower mounted a valiant defence before the Essex, on which he was serving as a midshipman, was taken. At the age of twelve, Farragut experienced something unprecedented in the annals of great sea commanders: he did not hear another shot fired in combat until he was older than sixty.

The history of war proves that he was right when he said, "I consider it a great advantage to obtain command young," adding that "having observed, as a general rule, that persons who come into authority late in life shrink from responsibility and often break down under its weight," his own career was a shining exception. It was not a belated step for Farragut to become a commander in the US Navy during peacetime; at forty years of age, he achieved the highest rank then available in the service.

Fourteen years later, he became a captain. Farragut was named to the Brooklyn Commission not long after receiving a promotion. She was one of six newly finished steam sloops-of-war, and the day he assumed command was the first time he had set foot on the decks of a modern-powered warship. The Brooklyn had wooden construction. She maintained a broadside configuration with her batteries, which consisted of nine-inch smooth-bore Dahlgren guns. She also added one or two pivot guns, which had a wide traverse, as their name suggests.

Despite being screw-driven, the Brooklyn class had fully fitted sails. At her finest, she could reach eight knots using just the engines. As the Civil War erupted in 1861, Farragut found himself in a challenging circumstance. He was living with his wife in Norfolk, Virginia, on half pay while ashore. Despite coming from a Southern family—his father lived in Louisiana in his final years—he had no roots in the region. He had been a faithful employee of the federal government for all of his active years. Farragut relocated to New York because he didn't like the political atmosphere in Norfolk. There, he was selected for active command and elevated to the rank of admiral.

Throughout the entire war, one of the missions assigned to the Federal Navy was to blockade the Gulf of Mexico. The secessionists maintained constant communication with their numerous supporters in Europe from these ports, especially New Orleans, and they exported cotton, which provided them with the weapons of mass destruction. Its navy proved to be a valuable asset to the Union throughout the conflict through the capture or sinking of Confederate commerce-destroyers, sometimes under the command of Englishmen. The greatest accomplishment of Farragut was taking New Orleans, which he attacked from the sea in April 1862.

He had demonstrated exceptional vigour and confidence for a man his age even before the procedures started. Using the Hartford, a ship like the Brooklyn, as his flagship, he quickly began to think in terms of the previous admirals due to his active service aboard experience. His words appear to repeatedly mirror Nelson's. Nelson's statement prior to the assault on New Orleans states that "the flag officer, having heard all the opinions expressed by the different commanders, is of the opinion that whatever is to be done will have to be done quickly." Farragut had extraordinary success. He began by sailing up the 140-mile Mississippi Estuary in an attempt to bypass the German cannons and get towards New Orleans. Ultimately, on the evening of April 24, he arrived at the forts that were protecting the area. Suddenly, fire-rafts descended upon the Hartford and ignited her, sending flames shooting from the exposed ports and forcing soldiers from their weapons. Boys, don't run from the fire! "There's a hotter fire than that waiting for those who don't do their duty," declared Farragut. Give that rascally tug a go.' The tug was driven off, attempting to force the fire-raft harder against the Hartford, and by daybreak, Farragut had passed through and was headed to the capital of Louisiana.

After his victory, he wrote to his wife, "It is a strange thought." 'I am here among my relatives and yet no one has dared to say ' ' I am happy to see you." ' As he had often said before, if he had to fight, he would rather it had been against his earlier foes, the British, than against his own people. Farragut's final and in some ways most remarkable service was his conduct of the operations against Mobile.

The port stood on the left bank of the estuary of the Mobile and Alabama rivers, not much more than 150 miles from New Orleans as the crow flies, and second in importance to it as a centre of Confederate maritime activity. Farragut had favoured an attack immediately after his first success, but other Federal preoccupations did not admit of this, and it was chiefly the threat of a new Confederate iron-clad, the Tennessee, known to be ready, that decided the attack. Farragut made a preliminary reconnaissance of the forts on 20 January 1864, and considered that with one supporting iron-clad he could clear the shipping in the bay, and that he could then reduce the forts at leisure, with the help of about 5,000 soldiers.

Six months passed, during which the Tennessee was moved to a point where she could threaten an assaulting force. Like the Merrimac before her, her strength lay in sloping armoured sides. She had six long-range rifled guns, but she suffered from the weakness of her predecessors in slow speed - six knots at best - and her rudder chains were exposed. She was fitted with a beak for ramming. Farragut, during these months of waiting, was at work administering the whole force engaged on the blockade. 'I have been down here within two months of five years,' he wrote, in words which again recall Nelson's while on watch off" Toulon, 'and recently six months on constant blockade off 'this port, and my mind on the stretch all the time.'

He was depressed, as were so many Federal officers, by the protracted resistance of the South, but he never contemplated even the idea of defeat. He wrote, "Any man who is ready for defeat would be half defeated before he started." Regarding his theory of warfare, he said, "Everything has a weak spot, and the first thing I try to do is find out where it is, pitch into it with the biggest shell I have, and repeat the dose till it operates." Eventually, in July, iron-clad monitors started to arrive. I hope for success, shall do all in my power to secure it, and trust in God for the rest. Two of them, the Tecumseh and the Manhattan, were seagoing and had a single turret armed with two 15-inch guns, the largest afloat, making them prime targets for the attack.

The Winnebago and Chickasaw were the other two river monitors. They were constructed in St. Louis to be used on the Mississippi. With four tiny screws and a light draft, they carried four 11-inch cannons arranged in two turrets. Mobile's main fortifications were Fort Morgan, which had 38 heavy guns; Fort Jackson, which had 27, and Fort St. Philip, which had 21 heavy guns, in addition to the Tennessee and three wooden gunboats. Fort Gaines was located on an island to the left of the approach, and there were obstacles in the way of Fort Morgan and Fort Gaines, including mines and fixed torpedoes. Farragut chose to move in two columns: one with the wooden vessels chained two by two, and the other with the ironclads.

The admiral required a west wind, if at all possible, to blow the smoke of battle into the eyes of Fort Morgan's defenders and a flood tide to help a damaged vessel past the forts. Again using language similar to Nelson's, Farragut wrote to his wife on August 4, the day of the planned attack, saying, "I write and leave this letter for you." If God is my leader, as I believe He is, and I put my trust in Him, I'm heading to Mobile first thing in the morning. I'm willing to bow to His will in that matter, as well as everything else, if He determines that this is the right spot for me to pass away.

The Tecumseh, the final of his monitors, reached the forts the same evening that he wrote, just as troops were prepared to occupy the forts. Farragut called his servant at three in the morning to check on the wind. It was useful. "We'll head out early in the morning," Farragut stated. Half past six, the Brooklyn, Farragut's former vessel, took the lead in the formation. The flagship trailed behind, with the Metacomet gunboat moored to her port side. The cannons of Fort Morgan fired just after seven o'clock. Farragut stood in the main rigging of the Hartford, presumably an uncommon posture for a flag commander in combat, to get the best possible view of the activities.

Standing next to him were the pilot and the captain of the Metacomet, who were on the main deck of the Hartford, allowing them to see well through the smoke. Farragut ascended as the smoke got thicker and higher, until coming to rest just below the pilot. Drayton, the flag captain, sent a seaman up with a flogging after growing concerned for the admiral's safety. The sailor said he had better make himself quick if the admiral would stand there. The monitors and wooden vessels in the two columns were getting closer to the entrance to the narrow channel and the mines. The Tecumseh was holding her fire for Tennessee. Farragut later said, "I thanked him for his consideration and took a turn around and over the shrouds and around my body for fear of being wounded, as shots were flying rather thickly." Then catastrophe struck. The pilots of Tecumseh and Brooklyn started to question the safe channel's alignment, putting their columns at risk of disarray and beneath Fort Morgan's artillery.

With her sights set on another Monitor and Merrimac duel, the Tecumseh appeared to be heading straight for Tennessee when she unexpectedly hit a torpedo. From his elevated position, Farragut saw her stumble and fall, putting her head down and turning her screws until she vanished. He continued to stand. With her engines at a sluggish speed and her bows pointing towards the fort, the flagship passed the Brooklyn, still confused, and her skipper yelled that torpedoes were up ahead. From his lofty position, Farragut yelled, "Damn the torpedoes, Captain Drayton, go ahead! Farragut was quite justified in his determination to hang on. That's right—torpedoes were present; the Hartford could hear them tapping at the bottom and primers breaking—but none of them burst.

After exchanging gunfire and making a fruitless attempt to ram the Tennessee, the Tennessee withdrew beneath the guns of Fort Morgan, while the Hartford and the other ships managed to pass through without incident. Buchanan gave up three hours after the fort opened fire, having gone forward by himself to engage the Union ships in combat. He was so pounded and slammed that he had no choice but to resign, his ship so badly damaged, and his guns rendered unusable. Thirteen of the three hundred and thirty-five Union soldiers who lost their lives in the iron hull of Farragut were lying coffined in the harbour after the victory of Mobile. They were highly esteemed by both his fellow citizens and the people of Europe. His humble but sure faith in himself had been as well-founded as his trust in Providence.

Although he was not able to participate in fleet operations, he can still be considered a complete sea commander because of his strategic and tactical acumen, his perseverance, and the love and assurance with which he led his fleet. The career of Farragut sheds light on several constants in sea power and attributes that have set the great admirals apart over the ages. The first of these was his complete knowledge of his line of work; the second was his capacity for planning and his ability to wait patiently; the third was his quick thinking in the face of danger and his bravery to continue.

This is not the same as being reckless or even naturally brave; rather, it is the capacity to assess the pros and cons, the enemy's true power and morale, and the will to stand by one's own side in the face of an immediate threat. At Copenhagen, Nelson demonstrated just how many of these qualities he possessed, just as Farragut did at Mobile. During Farragut's approach, there was a moment just before the Tecumseh struck the explosive block and just after she went down when a lesser man would have faltered, allowed his already shaky advance to spiral into disarray, and been forced to back down. The American Navy has never forgotten Farragut's famous line, "damn the torpedoes," which was so Nelsonian in its perspective and so appropriate in handling a difficult mission.

This is understandable, given that Farragut set an example for any aspirant sea officer to follow. Admiral Mahan, who wrote the most comprehensive seaman's biography of Nelson, was well within his rights to pay tribute to his esteemed colleagues, many of whom he served alongside. At the time of

Mobile, Farragut was sixty-three years old. It's noteworthy to note how old he was in relation to other admirals during the same years of their accomplishments. At the Four-Days' Battle, Monck was fifty-eight years old, while de Ruyter was one year older. When Duquesne went up against the legendary Dutchman, he was sixty-six years old. At the start of his lengthy series of fights in the Indian Ocean, Suffren was two years older than Hawke, who was fifty-four when he emerged victorious at Quiberon.

When he emerged victorious at the Glorious First of June, Lord Howe was nearly seventy years old, while Nelson was just forty when he emerged victorious at the Nile. The lessons from the years of sail warfare are few, but one should remember that a man with "fire in his belly" would probably never go out as long as his country needed him. As the years went by, he was probably going to become less determined in the area where younger men had been known to falter: in the task of maintaining a constant watch and guard that exhausts both ships and soldiers alike yet shuts off an adversary's ports and diminishes their initiative.

The American Civil War's Naval Battle of Mobile Bay, fought on August 5, 1864, was a pivotal moment in the Union's effort to seize control of the Gulf of Mexico and cut off the Confederacy's supply routes. For the belligerents involved, the impact of this conflict had far-reaching immediate and long-term effects. The Union's victory at Mobile Bay had important strategic ramifications in the short term. Following the naval battle, the Confederacy successfully locked off the port of Mobile, one of the last significant ports on the Gulf of Mexico that it controlled, by capturing Fort Morgan.

This triumph was essential to the Union's Anaconda Plan, which sought to control the Mississippi River and blockade the ports of the southern states in order to economically starve them. The Confederate economy and capacity to continue the war suffered a serious hit with the loss of Mobile as a commerce and blockade-running port. The Union's dominance over Mobile Bay economically hampered the Confederacy's commerce routes, especially with European countries. The inability to purchase war supplies and sell cotton further strained the Southern economy, which was already in trouble.

The Union's triumph strengthened their embargo and strengthened their hold on the war's economic resources, which helped to undermine the Confederate states as a whole. The strategic importance of the Battle of Mobile Bay and the audacity of Union Admiral David Farragut's leadership have made it a famous battle in military history. His well-known command to "Damn the torpedoes, full speed ahead!" has come to represent bravery and resolute leadership in the face of peril.

The engagement illustrated the value of naval superiority during the Civil War and the efficacy of Union naval strength. The conflict had important long-term ramifications as well. It raised spirits in the North and helped President Abraham Lincoln win re-election later that year. By undermining the Confederacy's resources and morale, the Union's win at Mobile Bay and other victories accelerated the end of the Civil War. In summary, the Naval Battle of Mobile Bay was a pivotal moment in the Civil War with significant historical, political, and economic ramifications. It was more than just a military conflict. It significantly hindered the Confederate war effort and was essential to the Union's victory. As a monument to naval might and strategic genius, the battle's legacy endures today.

11. Jutland, 1916 (5th Place)

The British and maybe the majority of the German public anticipated a full-scale naval war in the early days of World War I, possibly in the first few days of the conflict. They waited for almost two years, and when the moment finally arrived, the outcome was unclear and disheartening to the fleet. Given that they used fewer soldiers and caused more casualties than they suffered, the Germans declared a tactical win. The British quickly ascertained that the overall strategic outlook remained unaltered. They continued to dominate at sea, and they were aware that the German High Seas Fleet would not be the method of defeat. Indeed, the German High Command soon resorted to an alternative form of warfare: unrestricted submarine attacks, and they achieved some degree of success in this regard.

From these early, smaller-scale surface confrontations, the Germans had learned two important lessons. First, following an action in the Heligoland Bight in August 1914, they confronted Vice-Admiral Sir David Beatty, a leader skilled in battlecruiser tactics who was prepared to employ his large ships in a manner akin to that of a cavalry general. The second was that they needed to better safeguard their ships' magazines after an incident off the Dogger Bank the following year that resulted in the loss of the Blucher.

Important actions were performed. German strategy against a numerically superior British fleet was to trap a portion of it, most likely the battle-cruiser force, and destroy it before the British Commander-in-Chief, Admiral Sir John Jellicoe, could make an appearance. When Scheer assumed command of the German fleet in the early months of 1916, this was the strategy. He was under pressure to defend the navy's continued existence given the German army's sacrifices prior to Verdun. Scheer came up with two procedures. One was to immediately bombard a British east coast port, much like previous ones had done. Vice-Admiral von Hipper would use his battle cruisers for this mission, with Scheer providing cover and submarines positioned off the bases of the Grand Fleet.

Favourable weather conditions would be required, as would the assistance of Zeppelin airships. The third plan called for Hipper to stage a raid on British shipping off the coast of Denmark, once more with Scheer providing backup and submarines waiting in readiness. Submarines began to occupy their designated places for the first phase on May 15. However, inclement weather caused the airships to be grounded until May 30, at which point the submarines were almost scheduled to return. In order to ensure that Hipper's presence was publicised, he was instructed to travel to the Skagerrak and showcase himself along the Norwegian coast, while Scheer remained covertly out of sight on the Jutland shore. With knowledge of a major project underway, the British Admiralty ordered Jellicoe to set sail covertly on May 30. Scheer had no idea how big the whole force he would likely face when he set out because airship reconnaissance had not been feasible.

However, Jellicoe was unaware that the entire High Seas Fleet was assisting Hipper since he had effectively tricked the

British into thinking he was still in the River Jade. The ensuing conflict is among the most intricate in recorded history. This is hardly shocking, considering that it started with a double deception and continued in weather so unpredictable that, even though about 250 ships of all kinds were involved — 150 under Jellicoe's command and 101 under Scheer's — it was a unique occasion when more than a handful of ships at a time could track the movements of their own main forces or obtain more than a hazy glimpse of the enemy.

Without the use of radar, the fact that a Zeppelin was flying over the battlefield at a great height and completely unconscious of the fighting going on below her serves as the best example of the situation at the time. One of the last large-scale naval battles in which guns were crucial was Jutland. Airships, seaplanes, submarines, mines, and torpedoes were all present or close by, but none of them had a significant impact, and the British seaplane carrier Eugadine — the first of a class of ships that would later play a crucial role in history — was actually used to tow a damaged cruiser! An incident that happened when Scheer was still forty miles south of Hipper and Jellicoe was more than fifty miles north of Beatty set off the events.

Hipper's light cruisers headed to look into a steamship that was neutral. The scouts from Beatty shocked them with their quest. Along with six battle-cruisers — the Lion, Princess Royal, Queen Mary, Tiger, New Zealand, and Indefatigable — Beatty also had four new battleships — the Barham, Warspite, Malaya, and Valiant — under Sir Hugh Evan-Thomas. Without waiting to see if Evan-Thomas had picked up on his smoke-obscured signals, Beatty decided to pursue, and by the time the battleships caught up to him, the distance between him and his assistance had grown significantly.

Leading the way south at breakneck pace beside Hipper were Lutzow, Derfflinger, Seydlitz, Moltke, and von der Tann. Beatty charged into the trap that Scheer had set for him. Beatty held off on firing longer than necessary because the weather provided readings on the British internments that were much outside of their true range. His early salvoes fell well beyond Hipper when he opened fire, but his own ships were visible against the western sky. Beatty paid a high price for his sprint south.

Not too long after the explosions of the Indefatigable and Queen Mary, Beatty's flagship barely avoided the same fate. As one of her commanders observed, the armoured roof of a turret on the Lion "folded back like an open sardine tin," and the only thing that kept the ship afloat was the Major of Marines' decision to flood the turret's magazines before he died. 'Something looks amiss with our bloody ships today! Beatty shouted to his flag captain. There was, after all, but the admiral did not waver in his resolve to hunt down and, if feasible, eliminate the enemy. By now, Evan-Thomas, slicing corners, was fully on board, and documents indicate that the Germans were hit hard and often, albeit with relatively little catastrophic damage. The most significant came from a flotilla torpedo attack that struck the Seydlitz and had Hipper veer away.

Commodore Goodenough signalled to Beatty that he had spotted the enemy's main force at 4:33. Beatty pivoted to face the stated location. It took two minutes for the Lion to show the lengthy array of Scheer's battleships, which were twelve miles away. After Hipper's torpedo attack, Beatty used the opportunity to head northward towards Jellicoe after realising the nature of the trap. Beatty took on the duty of ensuring that Jellicoe would benefit from the meeting of the main fleets. This included preventing Hipper from spotting the Grand Fleet and alerting Scheer to the trap he was about to fall into. It was Beatty's turn to turn, and Evan-Thomas took heavy fire from Scheer and Hipper, although all of his ships managed to stay in the queue. Six columns abreast, Jellicoe's fleet had been advancing south while the battlecruisers were in combat. Jellicoe would have to go ahead of the pack in order to maximise his firepower. Which flank is he going to deploy on?

Much depended on his choice, but he had no idea how the Germans were feeling or where they were heading. Nelson had approached the battle of Trafalgar at a walking pace, with the enemy constantly visible. Under cover of darkness, Jellicoe and Scheer approached each other at Jutland at a combined forty to fifty knots; the enemy's precise composition was still unclear. Beatty had just broken off a second action, in which he had surged across Hipper's bows and forced him to retreat under cover of Scheer's guns, when Jellicoe and Beatty joined forces. Hipper threatened to launch a destroyer assault, but the Grand Fleet's abrupt appearance of more capable ships thwarted his plans.

The combined miscalculations of Beatty's Lion and Jellicoe's flagship Iron Duke when the British forces collided totalled eleven miles; also, at 6:14 p.m., Beatty was only able to report, "Enemy battle fleet bearing south east," since he had momentarily lost visual contact with the enemy. After that, Jellicoe ordered the formation of a line of combat on the port wing, moving southeast by southeast to keep the Germans and their coast at bay. Upon the completion of Jellicoe's manoeuvre, a vast array of battleships reached the horizon, constituting the most potent naval force the world had ever witnessed. As Scheer persisted, the full force of the British Fleet's weaponry soon overtook him. There didn't seem to be a way out of the devastation after he had run straight into the trap.

He subsequently reported, "The arc that stretched from north to east was a sea of fire." At this point, four of Hipper's five battlecruisers had suffered significant damage, so he quickly moved his flag from the Lutzow to the Moltke. With catastrophe staring him in the face, the German supreme commander pulled off a daring escape that was so well-hidden by smoke screens and torpedo strikes from his destroyer flotillas that the British were unaware of the exact details until the war was over. All German battleships underwent a simultaneous and total 180-degree turnabout at this time. At the precise time when failure appeared certain, Scheer executed the manoeuvre that he had trained for against this specific scenario.

Scheer had already made one escape, but later in the day, as it continued its beautiful south-easterly advance, he had to make two course changes to avoid Jellicoe's fleet. Scheer's "battle-turn" saved him a second time. The already damaged battlecruisers received a frantic signal to "charge the enemy" during his second major moment of danger, which led him to order his destroyers to assault behind a smoke screen. Ram. Ships are to be assaulted with little thought to the repercussions! By 7.20, Scheer had completed his withdrawal, and although Jellicoe had changed his course to the west in order to avoid torpedoes, David Beatty, 1st Earl Beatty, remained in contact and provided information about the German position.

At 8:17, Hipper's battlecruisers were visible once more, and Beatty fired at a distance of 10,000 yards. The last intact turret of the Deijflmger was rendered inoperable before the Germans could evacuate, and the Princess Royal's ranges were clear of the Lion's smoke for the first time since the fight began. The combat began with British big-gun salvoes fired by Beatty's ships, and it concluded with their firing. Jellicoe started night stations at dusk. He wanted to prevent his large ships from mistaking one another for the enemy by keeping his divisions in close formation. Now, his top priority was to stop Scheer from reaching the east and making his way back home. The van had Beatty stationed inside. Light cruisers and flotillas trailed after the battleships, which were arranged in three columns abreast in the centre.

In his quest to restore the security of the German minefields, Scheer had three options: heading southwest to reach the Ems; heading south-east to reach Horn Reef and the Elbe; or heading south-west to Heligoland and Wilhelmshaven. It would have been an invitation to disaster to try to use the Skagerrak to get back to the Baltic. Though Jellicoe sent a minelayer to block the south-easterly passage, he concluded that the Germans would move south despite some indication that Scheer would use the Horn Reef canal. Scheer followed this course, and although he lost one ship to the mines, he managed to sever Jellicoe's fleet's rear during the night and withdraw without incident. Even though there had been intense fighting during the night among the flotillas, Jellicoe was remarkably unaware of it.

Only at daybreak did he realise how much he had lost, and heading north towards his homeland, he found himself in charge of a battlefield bereft of anything but rafts and wreckage. In addition to explosives, other weapons are used in war, and the Germans, who arrived at the harbour first, received the news first, shocking the British people. The German battle fleet had sunk the Invincible, which was ahead of Jellicoe's main force, together with Queen Mary and the

Indefatigable. These casualties represented indisputable British losses. They also sank eight destroyers and three cruisers. More slowly, the German losses came to light: four light cruisers, four destroyers, one battleship, and one battle cruiser.

Unknown until much later, just six of Scheer's battleships managed to leave without damage, some of which were rather critical, while 26 of Jellicoe's battleships remained undamaged. With 6,000 British and 2,500 Germans lost, the human cost was more disproportionate than the number of ships lost. There were plenty of Germans saved from their damaged ships, but very few people on the three British battleships made it out alive. Churchill once said that Jellicoe was the only man who could have lost the war in a single afternoon. He had far more at stake than Scheer, and he was taking no chances since the fate of the Allies rested, at last, on the preservation of British sea supremacy. His war was one of the greatest battles ever fought.

Uncertain visibility, poor signals, overly centralised control, persistent smoke, and ship design flaws all hindered him. He had no idea that the High Seas Fleet would never present him with the same opportunity that had escaped him, but it did happen, and Beatty, his successor, had much worse luck. Jutland's naval action has generated more disputes than any other in history. The body of work is bitter, politicised, and always growing. Nothing can hide the fact that Jellicoe had three possible moments to make a fabricated decision: the first time he deployed the Grand Fleet; the second time Scheer ran into him; and the last time he thought about and disregarded the advice he had received just before midnight, which suggested that the Horn Reef was the most likely route by which the enemy would return.

The Churchillian remark was, "Three times is a lot." The heavy and tragic obligations that Sir John Jellicoe carried out throughout his two years of steadfast command, he continued, "are claims to the nation's lasting respect that are unassailable." However, the Royal Navy needs to identify the golden threads that preserved the bold and victorious customs of the past during the Great War in other people and situations. Despite this, it is nonetheless important to note that Jellicoe provided his subordinates with a model of a scientific naval officer. Among those closest to him, no leader has evoked greater affection than him. One of the biggest naval engagements in history took place during World War I, from May 31 to June 1, 1916, when the Imperial German Navy's High Seas Fleet and the British Royal Navy's Grand Fleet engaged in combat. Its aftermath and results shaped the naval combat of World War I and had a long-lasting effect on military history, with major strategic and economic ramifications for both Britain and Germany.

Following the match, both teams declared themselves winners. The German fleet did more damage than the British, but it was unable to break the British naval blockade or seriously undermine the Royal Navy's supremacy in the seas. The British incurred greater losses in terms of soldiers and ships. This impasse in strategy had far-reaching effects. Realising the power of the Royal Navy and the impossibility of breaking through the British blockade, the German High Seas Fleet was less likely to fight another major naval engagement of this magnitude. Due to this, German naval strategy changed to emphasise unrestricted submarine warfare. This decision would have a significant impact on the war, including the 1917 entry of the United States.

The British naval blockade proved to be economically effective after the Battle of Jutland. Germany, which was already experiencing a lack of resources, saw its condition get worse. The blockade made it extremely difficult for Germany to import necessities, which increased economic pressure and caused misery for the populace. These factors eventually stoked social unrest and political instability in post-war Germany. The battle marked the shift in military history from conventional naval combat to the more advanced, technologically advanced naval conflicts of the 20th century. It demonstrated the capabilities and constraints of dreadnought battleships as well as the value of fleet coordination, naval intelligence, and signalling. The fight also illustrated the growing importance of submarine warfare and naval aviation, which would eventually take centre stage in naval strategy in the years that followed the conflict. Jutland has important long-term ramifications. It confirmed the Royal Navy's dominance of the North Sea, which was important to the British since it guaranteed the blockade's continuation, which ultimately led to Germany's defeat. In summary, the naval action of Jutland was a critical point in naval history. Although Germany did not win the action outright, the result caused a strategic re-evaluation that would have a significant effect on the rest of World War I. Its results influenced both short-term tactical choices and long-term strategic planning, which in turn affected the path of World War I. The outcome of the conflict bears witness to the dynamic character of naval warfare and its pivotal function in moulding global affairs. The Imperial German Navy demonstrated its prowess and combat capabilities in this pivotal naval engagement of World War I, although Britain maintained dominance at sea.

12. Lepanto, 1571 (4th Place)

It is possible that sea battles are excellent for demonstrating the seaman fighter at his most skilled or determined. Sea battles may be neutral and even indecisive as engagements, but they are significant in their effect. Alternatively, sea battles may be both. The fight of Lepanto, which was the first sea battle of the western world to be honoured by artists of distinction, was one that was tremendous in every sense of the word. Over the course of the arduous and drawn-out conflict between the forces of Christendom and those of Mahomet, this event marked a significant advancement. It was a battle that took place on October 7, 1571, in the waters that separate Thessaly and the Morea, and it was a significant event in the history of Europe.

The primary fleet of the Turks, which was led by Ali Pasha, was beaten by a fleet that was comprised of the armies of the Holy League of Spain, the dominions of the Pope, and the Republic of Venice. All of these forces were under the direction of Don John of Austria. On the side of the victor, important leaders included the Spaniard Marquis de Santa Cruz, Andrea Doria, who led a Genoese squadron, and Marco Antonio Colonna, who commanded the soldiers of Pius V. In reality, the company was comprised of individuals from the majority of Catholic Europe, with the exception of France.

As a result of the fact that Lepanto occurred six years after the Turkish army had been defeated during the siege of Malta, it was able to ensure that the Mediterranean Sea would not be transformed into a lake characterised by the presence of Muslims. The only further Muslim expansion into Europe, which they had invaded with such success, would be at the expense of Poland and Russia, according to a portion of a fresco by Andrea Vicentino that is currently hanging in the Doge's Palace in Venice. The fresco depicts in graphic detail the hand-to-hand fighting that characterised this battle.

Although the outcome of this battle was slow to become apparent, the fresco depicts the hand-to-hand fighting that characterised this battle. And it would be by land. The Spaniards and Italians, with the example of the Knights of Malta in front of them, demonstrated that with leadership, bravery, and the assistance of a new weapon, in this case the heavily-gunned galleass, they were able to beat the traditional system of warfare that consisted mainly of oared galleys that were manned by slaves.

Don John of Austria, who had not yet reached the age of twenty-five when the Battle of Lepanto took place, had already distinguished himself in his military service against the Moors in Granada. He was the natural son of Emperor Charles V, who was married to a Bavarian woman named Barbara Blomberg. He was therefore the half-brother of Philip II of Spain, who was one of the supporting members of the Alliance, and he had been the primary admiral of Spain for a considerable amount of time, at least in name. Being fair-haired and thirsty for renown, Don John proved to be an effective leader for a fleet that was diverse and prone to conflict. After the recent loss of the majority of Cyprus to the

Turks, the Venetians, under the command of Augustino Barbarigo and the seasoned Sebastian Veniero, were in shock.

Furthermore, they had no affection for the Genoese, who were their long-standing adversaries at sea. Giovanni Andrea Doria, the nephew of one of Genoa's greatest men, was in charge of the Genoese forces. In Doria's squadron, there was a Spanish volunteer who was serving, and his fame was going to surpass even that of the commanders. Before he became the author of Don Quixote, he was known as Miguel de Cervantes. The Alliance was established in May of 1571 as a result of the arduous efforts of Pope Pius V. Its objective was to halt the territorial expansion of the Turks by sea and to prevent the deterioration of the African powers of Algiers, Tunis, and Tripoli by the use of a combined fleet.

Messina was going to be the location of the initial meeting. Upon his arrival, Don John discovered that he was in charge of more than three hundred ships, two-thirds of which were referred to as royal galleys. Each of these ships had a nominal complement of one hundred troops, in addition to the rowers who supplied the motive power. Eighty galleys, twenty-two more vessels, and at least twenty-one thousand fighting men made up the massive Spanish contingent, which was the greatest of the three. There were over a hundred warships that were given by the Venetians; nevertheless, they were poorly staffed.

The heavily armed galleasses that Francesco Bressano created were actually the Republic's most valuable asset. These galleasses, which lighter vessels brought into battle, were under the command of patricians who had sworn never to refuse to engage in combat with fewer than twenty-five opponents. In addition to having a beam that was wider than that of the galley, the galleass also had an additional depth that made it possible to construct a structure that was equipped with swivel guns. This structure was an early example of the modern armoured turret. In the galleass, the traditional beautiful stem of the galley was replaced with a menacing point, while lower down was a solid cutwater, which the heavy displacement of the vessel made effective against anything of smaller size that could not get out of the path.

Additionally, the sides and stern were heavily armed, and a deck that served as a platform for the combatants shielded the rowers. When they were engaged in combat, the rowers were yoked in both directions, with some of them pulling and others pushing at the fifty-foot oars. One of the key differences between the galleass oar and the galley oar was that the galleass oar featured slots that allowed the men to enter their fists. The oar itself was too huge to capture in its entirety. It was the Pope himself who outfitted twelve galleys, hired a great number of additional galleys, and provided the required men. At Messina, with his official approval, there was a gathering of at least eighty thousand troops. A total of approximately 50,000 individuals, including slaves, forced men, and volunteers, all worked at the oars.

The remaining individuals were members of the armed forces, and it was to representatives of the combatants that Don John, with the assistance of a blackboard, provided an explanation of his strategies. In addition to arranging the required signals, he provided his captains with comprehensive information on the manner in which he would respond to the most likely tactical contingencies. At the same time that the admiral was conducting a survey and issuing orders for his fleet, he received information that the Turks, who were estimated to have assembled some 300 ships, were making their way through the Ionian Sea and attacking islands within it. The first specific word of the enemy arrived before the end of the month, when Don John anchored near the coast of Corfu.

The Christians, who had set sail on September 6th, were the first to get this information. He discovered that Ali Pasha had lately landed on the island, set fire to a few churches, and was unsuccessful in his attempt to subdue the citadel on the island. After that, he fled to the harbour of Lepanto, which was located a significant distance up the eighty-mile stretch of water that is now known as the Corinthian Gulf. During a Council of War, which, like many other councils of this kind, was marked by acrimony and conflict, those who advocated for immediate attack were the ones who emerged victorious.

These individuals included Don John himself, as well as Colonna, Barbarigo, and Santa Cruz. It was becoming late in the season, and the disparities between the Allies, which had been present from the beginning, were developing and becoming more apparent. In large part, the fact that Spaniards had to be enlisted in the Venetian ships in order to bring them up to strength was the primary reason why the Venetians and the Spaniards had already come to blows with each other. Off the coast of Cephalonia, on October 6th, a ship from Crete delivered news of the loss of Famagusta, the final stronghold in Cyprus, as well as the torture and death of its noble Venetian defenders.

There was a wave of fear that went throughout the Allies, and an emergency push into waters where it was known that the enemy was lurking was ordered. In addition, there was one other piece of news that was not entirely upbeat. It appeared that the ships of the Algerian corsair Uluch Ali, who had previously been a fisherman in Calabria and was well-known to many members of the Christian fleet, at least by reputation, had supported Uluch Ali Pasha. As was the case in prior naval conflicts, the fleets engaged in combat like armies in Lepanto. In addition to having a disciplined formation, their directives were military in nature, and their tactics were based on their previous experience.

As a result of the conflict between the generals and their soldiers, the sailors were able to transport the ships to the desired location. On the evening of October 6th, the Turks had a favourable wind blowing in their direction, and they moved westward in the direction of the Christians. It was at the beginning of the day on October 7 that the most powerful forces that had ever come into contact with one another at sea came into sight of one another at the entrance to what is now known as the Gulf of Patras, which is located to the west of the Gulf of Corinth. In the moments leading up to the formulation of his official line of battle, Don John issued two instructions. Removing the iron beaks that protruded ten to fifteen feet from the bows of some of the warships was the first step in the process.

No one should fire "until they are close enough to be splashed with the blood of an enemy," according to the second principle and recommendation. There was wisdom in both directions. To win the battle, it would not be by ramming but rather through close combat, in which the armour that the Spaniards wore, in conjunction with their arquebuses, could prove to be a decisive advantage. Barbarigo and his Venetians were assigned to the left wing of the ship, and Barbarigo himself sailed as close to the rocks and shoals that were located along the coast as he could, in the hopes that his flank would not be able to be turned. The person on the right was Andrea Doria.

There was a mixture of Genoese and papal galley cultures. The flagship of Don John was located in the middle of the area, and it was easily identifiable by its high carved poop and triple stern lights, as well as its green pendant at the forepeak and its Holy Standard hanging from the main top. Colonna and Veniero were located close to him. Under the command of Santa Cruz, there were 35 Spanish and Venetian galleys that were in reserve, ready to use their strength where it was most required. When the two fleets were getting closer to one another, the six Venetian galleasses that were going to be the spearheads of the Christian assault were hauled into position.

There were two posted in front of each main squadron, and they were in the queue ahead. Following the completion of all preparations, Don John boarded a swift watercraft and sailed along and behind the three-mile front that his forces extended. He was able to inspire his troops while simultaneously receiving cheers from them. Respect for their commander was at least a shared trait among the Allies, and their confidence in him was well-founded. Once Don John had made his way back to his galley, the wind had shifted in his favour, making it easier for him to sail. Even though he was now able to observe that Ali Pasha had his fleet arranged in the shape of a massive crescent, he quickly changed this configuration so that it was more in line with his own preferences.

Within the Turkish fleet, there were a significant number of Christian galley slaves. Ali Pasha addressed them and stated, "If I am victorious in the battle, I guarantee that you will be free." To the extent that the day is yours, then God has bestowed it onto you. The galleasses of the Allied Centre were the ones who performed the initial blood draw. They were able to use their guns, which were heavier than anything the Turks had, with such effectiveness that no adversary could come close to catching up with them. These individuals carried out their mission at a considerable distance, sinking a number of Turkish galleys even before the main forces came into contact with them. This initial setback was partially responsible for the separation of the left and right wings of the Muslim community from the core of the group.

In an effort to outflank Andrea Doria, Uluch Ali made a broad sweep towards the southern coast, and Mahomet Sirocco followed a similar course towards Barbarigo. Both of these guys were attempting to outflank Andrea Doria. The middle squadron of Ali Pasha, after evading the powerful galleasses to the best of its ability, continued on to meet those of Don John when it arrived. By midday or shortly after, the sword and scimitar had taken the place of the crossbow and the arquebus on the Turkish and Don John's flagships. The decks were slippery with blood from the close battle, and by that time, all three squadrons had successfully taken control of the situation. Mahomet Sirocco's strategy was successful on the Christian left because of his efforts.

Because of his familiarity with the coastline, he was able to sail even closer to it than Barbarigo did, making it possible for him to encircle him. In addition to being murdered by an arrow, the Venetian admiral was attacked by eight galleys, which ultimately resulted in his death. Two times, the flagship of the Venetian fleet was attacked, and both times, it was retaken. The ship that Mahomet Sirocco was captaining was finally sunk, and he was thrown into the water as a result of the assistance that Canale and other individuals provided. His captors decapitated him on the spot after rescuing him, despite the fact that he had already suffered severe wounds by that point.

In the beginning, the war had been just as disastrous for those on the Christian right. Uluch All had immediately doubled back to a gap that had appeared in the Allied line, and he had grabbed a portion of Don John's squadron in the rear. This was despite the fact that he had not been able to outflank Andrea Doria. One of the ships attacked was the Capitana of Malta, which Giustiniani, a Prior of the Order of St. John, was in command of. The Capitana was taken as a prize after the Prior was killed by five arrows that were embedded in his body. At the most crucial moment, Santa Cruz went to the rescue, seeing the Maltese in the hands of the enemy. Uluch Ali, also in a hurry to escape, gave up his captive and made a hasty retreat.

The outcome of the matter was decided in the middle. From the very beginning, it was abundantly evident that Don John's order to destroy the iron beaks was a good one. The forepeak of the Turkish flagship, which had been stripped of its long spur, towered over the rowing benches of his opponent, yet the forecastle cannons of his opponent fired into the air. When stationed at a lower level, those belonging to Don John were able to clear the Turkish galley with shots just below her water line. Additionally, the admiral was able to manoeuvre and close more easily than his opponent.

A number of boarding nets provided adequate protection for the bulwarks, and the armoured Spanish arquebusiers quickly devastated the Turkish ranks. It was not for nothing that the Spaniards were considered to be the most consistently reliable soldiers of their era. It was when Don John gave the order to board that the action reached its peak; teams were forced to retreat not once but twice, but in the end, they were able to carry the Turkish poop. Ali Pasha, who had already been hit in the head by a ball propelled by an arquebus, made an attempt to buy his life by promising him treasure in that location. It was a waste of time.

Even his protective talisman, which consisted of a crystal ball containing the right canine associated with Mahomet, was not of any use to him. A soldier cut him down, hacked off" his head, and carried it to Don John. The admiral, recoiling in horror, ordered the man to throw the grisly trophy into the sea; but he was disobeyed. The Spaniard mounted it on a pike, which was then held aloft on the prow of the Turkish flagship. Consternation spread among the Moslems, and, within a few moments, resistance was over.

The Ottoman standard, a sacred emblem inscribed with the name of Allah twenty-nine thousand times and never before lost in battle, was lowered from the maintop. All attempts at relief were repulsed cither by Don John or by the vigilant Santa Cruz, now returned from the rescue of the Capilana. Don John was then able to turn his attention to his right wing, where all was not well with Andrea Doria, who, for a time at least, was believed to have been the prisoner of one Occhiali. No less than five of Doria's galleys had been stricken.

The San Giovanni and the Piamontesa of Savoy were ships of the dead. The Doncella was in not much better case, while in the Florence, only the captain and seventeen seamen survived out of two hundred. The Marquesa was also hard pressed. It was in this ship that Cervantes was serving. He had been ill with fever before the battle, but he had risen from his sick-bed and had volunteered for a place of danger. There he remained throughout the battle, one of the wounds he received disabling his left hand for life. Uluch Ali, whose Algerians had done most of the damage on the Christian right, retreated to the shelter of the forts of Lepanto where he learnt of the death of Ali Pasha, but sixteen of his galleys doubled back upon their pursuers, and fought one of the bloodiest encounters of the entire day with Don Juan of Cardona, whose forces they outnumbered two to one. Of Cardona's five hundred Sicilian soldiers, only fifty emerged unharmed, Cardona himself being fatally wounded before the enemy were driven off.

Veniero and Colonna, Don John's companions of the centre, each fought nobly, and as the four-hour fight came to a close, with the enemy centre and right almost totally destroyed, and the left in gradual retreat, Don John at last had time to survey the action as a whole and to begin to reckon his gain and loss. Nearly 8,000 of the flower of Spanish and Italian chivalry had perished: double that number were wounded. The Turks and Algerians lost at least three times as many killed, and some twelve thousand Christian slaves were rescued from their galleys.

Never again did the Sultan contrive to assemble so powerful a fleet. Christians and Turks had been roughly equal in numbers, and they fought with equal courage. Victory went to the side with better weapons and better leadership, and in this respect the galleass, and the person of Don John, proved decisive. Lepanto was Don John's first and last major sea battle. He died in the Low Countries at the age of thirty-one, a man of one success and many disappointments. Like the galleys he commanded, he belonged to an old order of sea warfare, one whose history went back to the days of Actium, Salamis and beyond. The future was with sail, with the broadsides of the future ships of the line.

The Naval Battle of Lepanto, fought on October 7, 1571, between the Holy League, led predominantly by the Spanish Empire and the Papal States, and the Ottoman Empire, marked a pivotal moment in naval history. Its aftermath had profound strategic, economic, and cultural implications for both the victors and the vanquished, reshaping the balance of power in the Mediterranean. In the immediate aftermath, the Holy League celebrated a significant victory. The battle halted the Ottoman expansion into the Mediterranean, a strategic shift that had long-term implications.

For the Ottomans, the defeat at Lepanto was a major setback, but not a crippling one. They quickly rebuilt their fleet, maintaining their naval presence in the Mediterranean. However, the psychological impact of the defeat was substantial, diminishing the aura of Ottoman invincibility and bolstering the morale of Christian Europe. Strategically, Lepanto marked the end of Ottoman naval dominance in the Mediterranean. While they remained a significant sea power, their ambitions of expanding further westward were effectively curtailed.

For the Holy League, particularly for Spain and Venice, the victory at Lepanto solidified their naval supremacy in the region. This shift in naval power had significant economic implications. Control of Mediterranean trade routes, vital for the flow of goods and wealth, was now more securely in Christian hands. This control bolstered the economies of the Holy League's member states, particularly Spain and Venice, allowing them to exert greater influence over Mediterranean trade. Culturally, the battle had a lasting impact on both Christian and Muslim worlds. It became a symbol of Christian resistance against Ottoman expansion, celebrated in art, literature, and history. For the Ottomans, the defeat was a reminder of the limitations of their naval power and the need for continued military and technological advancements.

In military history, Lepanto is remembered as one of the last major engagements fought primarily between galleys and as a turning point in naval warfare, highlighting the transition towards more heavily armed and manoeuvrable sailing ships. The battle demonstrated the effectiveness of coordinated naval tactics and the importance of firepower and discipline in naval engagements. In conclusion, the Battle of Lepanto's outcomes had far-reaching consequences. It reshaped the naval power dynamics in the Mediterranean, had significant economic repercussions for the belligerents, and left a lasting cultural and military legacy. The battle's significance in naval history cannot be overstated, as it marked a turning point in the struggle for control of the Mediterranean and influenced the course of European and Ottoman histories.

13. Midway, 1942 (3rd Place)

In the same way that the Pacific Ocean is more powerful than any other ocean, the naval battles that took place between the United States and Japan in the aftermath of the attack on Pearl Harbour on December 1, 1994, took place in a manner that was reminiscent of the battle that took place at Port Arthur in 1904. These battles made preceding maritime wars appear to be relatively insignificant. There were enormous distances, forces that were deployed, and potentialities, and the element of air power was so dominant in the decisive naval combat that was conducted during the first year that surface contact and even submarine-and-surface contact became secondary. Because of the ease with which the Japanese were able to make their huge conquests, they had a strong desire to build a defensive perimeter through which they could consolidate their achievements.

The Japanese made the decision to expand their military reach even further outside, with plans that included the Aleutian Islands, Midway, Samoa, Fiji, New Caledonia, and Port Moresby. Additionally, they failed to take into account the nearly endless resources that the United States possessed. At the end of May 1942, they mounted their second assault against Midway Island, which is located 1,200 miles west-northwest of Hawaii. Their first attempt at the mission was unsuccessful at Port Moresby. The American countermeasure, which was greatly aided by the fact that the enemy code had been broken, consisted of moving the carriers Enterprise and

Hornet, which were commanded by Admiral Spruance, to Pearl Harbour as quickly as possible so that Admiral Fletcher's crippled Yorktown could be rebuilt.

The three carriers, along with eight cruisers and fourteen destroyers, were all under Admiral Fletcher's command and were making their way towards Midway by the end of the month. A total of fourteen submarines were disposed of west and north of Midway, with Admiral Nimitz, the Commander-in-Chief of the United States Pacific Fleet, making the decision to take general control of operations at Pearl Harbour. The Japanese would not have placed great importance on Midway because it only offered a shallow harbour and a small airfield. However, the United States would have been deprived of an advanced base that could have been valuable for the submarines that were already threatening Japanese supply lines.

Admiral Yamamoto made his way out to sea with the most powerful force he could muster, which included nine battleships, including the new Yamato, flying his flag, four carriers, cruisers, and destroyers, and transports carrying approximately 2,000 men. In preparation for the impending danger, Admiral Fletcher established a position around 200 miles to the north-northwest of the island on June 3rd. The Japanese came with three different groups of people. With all four carriers, two battleships, cruisers, and destroyers, Vice-Admiral Nagumo was leading the way towards the north. Despite the fact that their existence was not anticipated, his mission was to prevail over the shore-based aircraft of Midway as well as any opposition from carrier-borne planes that might be in the vicinity.

The transports, which had been escorted from the Marianas, arrived from the west-southwest direction. They were prepared to launch an attack on the island after the air opposition had succeeded. The battle fleet under Admiral Yamamoto was in support, and it was already powerful enough to eliminate the majority of surface troops and capitalise on success. Submarines were standing by at the approaches to Midway and on a line west of Hawaii, ready to report any actions taken by the United States. At nine o'clock in the morning on June 3, a flying boat was the first to notice the Japanese convoy. This saw the convoy for the first time.

However, Yamamoto now knew that the Americans had been informed, and he still intended to reach Midway without encountering more than local opposition. Nine Flying Fortresses moved up from Midway to strike, but all of their bombs missed, and a night attack by torpedo-carrying Catalinas scored just a tiny success when they attempted to attack. At the break of dawn on June 4, the Japanese carrier force had successfully arrived at a location around 200 miles north of Midway without being discoverable. With fifty fighters accompanying them, they launched one hundred bombers from that location. Even though he was still undetected, Admiral Fletcher was around 200 miles east-northeast of the Japanese at this time.

Almost immediately after that, the air patrols of Midway spotted the approaching strike, and then later, the carriers, and shortly after that, the combat was fairly engaged. First, fifteen flying fortresses that had been dispatched against the assault force were redirected towards the ships. Next, all Midway aircraft were flown away: fighters to meet the striking force, torpedo aircraft, and dive bombers to attack the carriers. Finally, all Midway aircraft were flown away. Everyone endured a significant loss. Even though the fighters were successful in bringing down some Japanese, it was not enough to prevent the Midway sites from being heavily hit. As a result of the absence of fighter defence, the aircraft that attacked the carriers sustained almost complete destruction. Despite the fact that Flying Fortresses delivered more than one hundred bombs from a height of twenty thousand feet without achieving a single hit, the situation appeared to be completely favourable to the Japanese.

Following this, a sequence of strokes and counterstrokes occurred, each of which served to exemplify the phrase "the fortunes of war." Finally, the Japanese were able to identify the existence of the American carriers, and they shifted their route to the north-east in order to get closer to the adversary while simultaneously utilising every aircraft that was available. As a result of prior reports, the United States of America dispatched one hundred aircraft at eight in the morning from the Enterprise and Hornet, while Yorktown was waiting in reserve.

After making the assumption that the Japanese were still making their way towards Midway, the Americans discovered that the anticipated enemy position was an empty sea. They did this without being aware of the Japanese's change of direction. Immediately after that, the dive bombers and fighters of the Hornet turned south, but they did not discover anything. They either arrived at Midway or ran out of fuel south of it. The torpedo-aircraft of the same ship made a chance discovery of the adversary, launched an attack, and were all quickly destroyed by the enemy. The dive bombers of the Enterprise also discovered the Japanese, but their fighters and torpedo aircraft arrived at them first.

The fighters were patrolling high overhead, waiting for the dive bombers, but they had to return because of a lack of fuel. When, therefore, the torpedo-aircraft and dive-bombers went in together from different directions at approximately ten in the morning, they would have been completely without fighter protection if it weren't for a further chance that brought the entire Yorktown strike, which occurred approximately an hour later than the others, to the same position at the same time. They were the dive bombers who were responsible for the damage. In spite of the fact that the Yorktown fighters were able to accomplish anything, twenty out of twenty-six torpedo aircraft were shot down, and there were no hits registered. The Japanese patrols focused their attacks primarily on torpedo aircraft, which were regarded as being both more dangerous and more susceptible.

Nevertheless, the dive-bombers were unopposed in the subsequent brawl, and they delivered blows that were so devastating that they pretty much won the fight. There were four bombs that penetrated the carrier Kaga, three bombs penetrated the Soryu, and two bombs penetrated the Akagi. Every one of the three ships experienced fires that were out of control, and they eventually came to a complete halt. An American submarine launched three torpedoes at the Sry during the afternoon, and she sank at dusk. The incident occurred in the afternoon. Only a short amount of time remained for Kaga and Akagi to live. Soon after noon, the Japanese launched an assault on the American carriers, with the majority of their assault focusing on the Yorktown carriers.

Three bombs were detonated, but the assailants were eliminated by gunfire. Although she was able to continue to steam at 19 knots, the damage to a ship that had already been mended was significant. The Hiryu, the only Japanese carrier

146

that was still in operation at the time, launched another assault on her not long after that. During the course of the battle, Yorktown was destroyed by two torpedoes, and an enemy submarine was able to finish off the ship while it was in tow.

A total of six bombs had been dropped on the Hiryu before dark, and the ship sank the next day. Even though the Americans were not yet aware of it, they had achieved a significant win despite having a force that was significantly smaller in size than the adversaries. They were successful in putting a stop to the expansion of Japan and had taken away two-thirds of the antagonist's large carriers. None of this was quite finished. Admiral Yamamoto, upon realising the magnitude of the disaster to his carriers, had already indicated a general retirement; however, he authorised a surface bombardment of Midway, half as a method to save face and half as a way to hide his withdrawal.

Three heavy cruisers, the Mogame and the A4ikuma, were involved in a collision while attempting to avoid colliding with an American submarine. The four cruisers had been escorting the transports prior to the collision. Following the abandonment of the operation, the cruisers headed back to their respective homes, with the Mogame leaving behind a trail of oil fuel. Enterprise and Hornet, two American aircraft carriers that were currently pursuing the Japanese, discovered the disabled cruisers on June 6 and proceeded to destroy them with their hammers. Despite the fact that she had an oil leak, the Mogame was able to make it to Truk, which was 2,000 miles away, despite the fact that the Mikuma had crashed.

The Americans, who were getting close to the end of their fuel supply, made their way back to Pearl Harbour, where they were greeted by Admiral Nimitz with the congratulations they had earned. This engagement marked the beginning of the turning of the tide of success for the Japanese. There might be difficulties for the United States in the future, but from this point forward, there was unquestionable evidence to support the belief that they would ultimately prevail. In particular, when viewed from the perspective of the Pacific Theatre of World War II, the Naval Battle of Midway, which took place from June 4 to June 7, 1942, is considered to be one of the most significant naval conflicts in the history of the world.

It was the aftermath of this fight that had far-reaching repercussions, both strategically and economically, for the United States of America and Japan. It altered the direction of the war as well as the balance of naval strength in the Pacific. Following the events that transpired, the United States Navy quickly established itself as the preeminent naval power in the Pacific. The Imperial Japanese Navy suffered a crushing blow as a result of the loss of four aircraft carriers, a heavy cruiser, and numerous other ships, as well as the considerable loss of trained pilots and staff. They also suffered damage to several additional ships.

This loss caused an irreversible shift in the balance of naval power in the Pacific, which swung in favour of the United States of America and its supporters. The victory at Midway put a stop to the Japanese advance in the Pacific, which prevented any more threats to Hawaii and other vital places. Additionally, it paved the path for the United States to launch offensive operations. When it came to the Pacific War, Midway was a pivotal milestone from a strategic standpoint. It brought a stop to the phase of Japanese expansion and marked the beginning of a period of offensives with American leadership. In order to capitalise on their triumph, the United States of

America launched a series of island-hopping missions, which ultimately brought them to the doorstep of Japan.

The conflict marked a change away from plans that were centred on battleships and underlined the crucial necessity of aircraft carriers in modern naval warfare. Within the realm of economics, the conflict had considerable repercussions. The loss of carriers and skilled staff was a tremendous blow for Japan, and their war industry had a difficult time recovering from the effects of this strike. With its massive industrial capacity, the United States, on the other hand, was able to more effectively replace casualties and continue to grow its naval and aviation forces, earning a decisive material edge on the battlefield.

It is common practice to consider Midway to be among the most significant naval battles in the annals of military history. Specifically, it highlighted the significance of intelligence, notably the ability to break codes, as well as the role that air power plays in naval conflicts. In addition, the combat brought to light the significance of strategic planning and the element of surprise, both of which were essential components of the final victory for the United States. In the aftermath of the Battle of Midway, the consequences were significant and long-lasting. This event was a crucial turning point in the Pacific War, as it substantially damaged the naval force of the Japanese, bolstered the morale of the American people, and strengthened their strategic position. The significance of the engagement rests in the fact that it served as proof of the superiority of air power in naval combat and played a significant role in determining the fate of World War II in the Pacific.

14. The Spanish Armada, 1588 (2nd Place)

There were a number of medals that were created in celebration of Lepanto, and many of them included the image of Philip II of Spain as one of the winners. Not only was he able to assert that his subjects had played a significant role in the eventual triumph over the Turks, but he could also assert that a member of his family had achieved the highest possible level of glory on that particular occasion. Seventeen years later, when he was planning his great "enterprise" against Elizabeth I's England, he was unable to command the services of either Don John or Santa Cruz because both of them had passed away. Furthermore, he himself, who was older and more experienced, had experienced a consistent sense of disappointment even in the maritime realm, where he had the ability to summon the most powerful forces associated with his age.

The Spanish Armada, which set sail from Spain in 1588, was the culmination of a war between England and Spain that had been maintained, both covertly and officially, over a period of many years, off the southern coasts of Europe and in Spanish territory on the other side of the Atlantic. However, it was not the final episode in this conflict. Philip had high hopes that his massive fleet, which would serve to carry an army from his territories in Flanders, would be the method by which he would be able to subjugate England, re-establish Catholicism within the country, and protect his overseas possessions from the ravages of daring explorers like Francis Drake. Because Philip's preparations against England had been so extensive and his men had been assembled so slowly, he offered his adversaries every opportunity to delay him.

To a great extent, they had been seized. During the month of April in the year 1587, Drake caused a great deal of chaos in both the inner and outer harbours of Cadiz. He had made a point of "singing the King of Spain's beard" by setting fire to the ship that was intended to carry the flag of his senior admiral. Then, he had relocated to the Azores, where he had successfully taken possession of the San Felipe, which was the most valuable prize that he had ever won. In spite of this, he made a statement that has since gained widespread recognition: "There must be a beginning to any great matter, but the continuing unto the end until it is thoroughly finished yields the true glory." It was impossible for that final day to arrive until the Armada had been beaten at sea after it had been ordered and constructed.

It was not until May of 1588 that the Spaniards were finally prepared, and the Duke of Medina Sidonia was assigned leadership of the Spanish forces. His experience and capabilities were not comparable to those of Santa Cruz; nonetheless, he was the King's cousin, his bravery was unquestionable, and everyone would obey him. Santa Cruz himself was a formidable opponent. His one hundred thirty ships were organised into principal squadrons, which included those from Portugal, Biscay, Guipuzcoa, Castille, Andalusia, and the Levant. It was the responsibility of the men-of-war to guard the transports that were transporting the troops that were going to join the troops assigned to the Duke of Parma in the Low Countries. When taken as a whole, the army would be unstoppable, a force that the fleet and warriors of Elizabeth would, according to Philp's calculations, be unable to overcome. In order to achieve his objective of capturing London, Medina Sidonia's plan was to first establish a stronghold in the Downs and then consult with Parma on the most effective way to launch an assault up the Thames.

The admiral was given orders to seize the Isle of Wight as a preliminary step before the major campaign. This was to be done in the event that the weather was difficult. Drake was of the opinion that the conflict should start as far away from the English coast as possible, preferably off and even inside the enemy's own harbours. This is a perspective that has been shared by every strategist since Drake's time. The following is an excerpt from what he wrote: "With fifty sails of shipping, we shall do better upon their own coast than a great many more will do here at home." As a result of the fallout, his plans did not meet with immediate approval, and Drake did not receive the position of top command in the English navy.

The individual who held the position of High Admiral, Lord Howard of Effingham, was given the instruction to embark in human form. With the prestige of state office, Queen Elizabeth believed that only a nobleman could wield the necessary influence over such disparate characters as Drake, Hawkins, and Frobisher. Similar to Philip, Queen Elizabeth believed that this was the only way to exercise such authority. There is no question that she was correct. Sir Walter Raleigh, who had initially given the ship the name Ark Royal after himself, had just lately sold it to the Crown. Howard flew his flag aboard the new galleon, Ark Royal. Drake received the position of Vice Admiral at Plymouth. The main army had been assembled by the 23rd of May, 1588, off the coast of the west country port. For the purpose of meeting Howard, Drake embarked on a journey with thirty ships, "making a brave show of his skill and diligence." Men shouted and saluted as trumpets sounded in the background. Howard presented Drake with a Vice Admiral's flag that he had flown from his own ship as a gift, and after that, everything went smoothly.

A contemporary stated that Drake "showed always one mind and thought with the senior admiral," despite the fact that there were many who had thought, or even feared, a different conclusion. The fleet that Elizabeth commanded comprised one hundred and two ships, ranging in size from the scouting pinnaces to the Frobisher's Triumph, which was capable of competing with any Spanish vessel. The Lion, the Tiger, the Dreadnought, the Victory, the flagship of Hawkins, and the Revenge, which wore Drake's flag as Vice-Admiral and which would go on to achieve additional distinction later, under Sir Richard Grenville, were among the ships that were among the famous names that were associated with them.

In addition to thirty-five royal ships, there were fifty-three more ships of a similar size that belonged to private owners. The majority of these ships were fully armed with artillery. This was a challenging supply. At each of the ports, there was a general lack of victuals, and there was also a lack of a significant reserve of powder and shot. Howard expressed his frustration by saying, "I do not know if there is a way to deal with the Mariners that would allow them to rest contentedly with sour beer." Despite this, he thought he was in charge of "the most gallant company of captains, soldiers, and mariners that I think anyone has ever seen in England." He continued with a cheery tone. In accordance with Drake's suggestion, Howard embarked on a voyage on the 30th of May with the intention of capturing the adversary.

There was no hope for him. While the Spaniards advanced into Corunna, the English were forced to return to Plymouth by the violent winds that blew over the summer. In spite of the fact that Howard went into the Bay of Biscay on two separate occasions, he never came across a hostile vessel. As a result of the strong south wind that pushed him in the direction of home on the second mission, the Armada was able to leave the port and begin its subsequent journey to the Channel. At the time when the Spaniards gained visibility off the coast of the Lizard, the English were already in port at Plymouth on the 19th of July. They were in a hard position to get a hold of an adversary who, far from having been damaged off his own beaches, was approaching with military discipline in what would have appeared to be overwhelming progress.

The wind was blowing from the west. There is no basis in reality for the narrative that Drake was playing bowls when he received the word that the enemy was upon him and that he said, "Play out the game; there's time for that and to beat the Spanish after." This legend has no basis in reality. In point of fact, if the English were to beat out of Plymouth Sound against the wind, every second was crucial, and not a single one missed the mark. Using the local knowledge and staying well within the shoreline, a few of Drake's ships were able to sail to the west of Medina Sidonia in a short amount of time.

By the morning of July 21st, the English and Spanish were in the relative positions that they would maintain, with some adjustments, for the days that would be crucial. In the beginning, Howard did not have his ships in any particular order; rather, they were positioned behind and to the windward of the slowly moving mass of his adversaries, of whom he mentioned that "the entire world had never seen such a force."

At night on the 20th of July, he had taken his main unit across the enemy front, and then he had tacked, passing the Eddystone Rock, to join the inshore forces that were already on Medina Sidonia's trail. In the secret order that Philip II of Spain delivered to Medina Sidonia, his Commander-in-Chief, prior to the launching of the Armada, he instructed Medina Sidonia to bring him down at any time at his own discretion. In spite of the fact that they had not yet fired a single shot, Howard and Drake had already attained a strategic advantage. This was a clear benefit for an aggressive leader. The Spanish had no intention of engaging in a massive military conflict at sea. They would have preferred to engage intimately, as Don John had done at Lepanto, if they had been obliged to do so due to the fact that they had tall ships and warriors who were well disciplined.

It was common knowledge that the English were fully aware of this fact, and they planned to take advantage of their convenient ships in order to maintain their distance and fire their guns at the greatest possible range. To close would have been a foolish decision. In addition to the fact that the Spanish ships were larger and had a stronger hull, there was a claim that the Spanish had lined the hulls of their ships with tar, wool, pitch, and other materials that they believed no shot could penetrate. We would be using cannons as our weapons of choice in this conflict. Philip wrote to his commander-in-chief, "You should see that your squadrons do not break their battle formations and that the captains, moved by greed, do not pursue the enemy and take prizes."

He further emphasised that the captains should not pursue the enemy and take prizes. As inexperienced as he was, Medina Sidonia remained steadfast in his adherence to these directions, and the manner in which he managed to keep his fleet together while it was travelling up the Channel was a source of admiration for the entire community. Considering that the Spaniards did not split up, the English had little choice but to harass them, which they did both during the day and at night.

However, by the time Howard had arrived at the Isle of Wight, he had already organised his ships into four divisions, each of which was led by himself, Hawkins, Frobisher, and Drake. Initially, they attacked in a manner that was not in any particular sequence, although Howard and Drake were constantly at the forefront of the battle. Typically, Drake was the recipient of one of the initial fortunate events. While he was in charge of the fleet, he noticed a galleon approaching from the direction of the horizon on the evening of Sunday, July 21.

The galleon's bowsprit and foremast were missing, indicating that she was certainly in trouble. separated from the rest of the Armada, who were present. The ship was known as the Nuestra Senora del Rosario, and it was the flagship of the Andalusians. Don Pedro de Valdes, the captain of the ship, was considered to be one of the most skilled sailors that Medina Sidonia had at his disposal. On the previous day, he had been involved in a collision with another vessel, and as a result, he was unable to keep up with the rest of the fleet. In the moments before dawn, Drake personally commanded de

Valdes to surrender, and he did so without putting up any resistance.

Drake invited him to join him on board the Revenge, and for a certain number of exciting days, he served as his charming host. She was the only vessel to be captured during the combat, with the exception of the San Salvadore, which was hauled into Weymouth following an internal explosion. The Rosario was sent into Dartmouth with a prize crew, and she was the only vessel to be captured throughout the conflict. When the fleets finally made their way out of Portland, the wind had already slowed down.

Despite the fact that fighting had been intermittent since the 21st, with more sustained action on the 23rd when a shift of wind favoured the Spaniards, who seized the opportunity to maul the Triumph, there had not yet been any decisive action fought. By Friday, the 26th, the sea was so calm and the enemy was so passive that Howard was able to summon his captains to the flagship. There, he exercised his delegated power to bestow a knighthood upon John Hawkins, Martin Frobisher, and several individuals, including Beeston of the Dreadnought, all of whom had demonstrated their prowess in action on the 23rd and 25th of July.

Richard Hawkins, John Hawkins' son, was also serving with the Fleet. The day that had passed had been primarily devoted to the storage of Howard's ships. On the evening of July 27, the wind picked up, and the Spaniards, who were "always before the English like sheep," manoeuvred their course towards Calais, which is where Medina Sidonia pulled the Armada to anchor. As a result of the fact that he had been unsuccessful in any attempt he might have made to seize control of the Isle of Wight, his immediate objective was to make contact with Parma, who was located in Bruges at the time. The following day, Howard was bolstered by a detachment from the Thames, which was led by Lord Henry Seymour and Sir William Winter.

He was aware that he would never have a greater chance of putting the Spaniards in a position where they were at a disadvantage. It was necessary to use fireships in order to force Medina Sidonia out of his anchorage before Parma got a chance to find out where he was. As a contemporary observer put it, eight of these destructive vessels were ranged in such a way that they came down with the wind and the night tide towards the dense mass of Spanish shipping, "spurting fire and their ordnance shooting, which was a horror to see." Guns were fired, sails were set, rudders were secured, and crews were removed.

In an instant, everything became a mess. There was nothing that was more dreaded than fire during days of sail, and it was soon every ship for herself, even with the disciplined men-of-war who, up until that point, had remained so carefully together. During the process of the warships making their way out to what they assumed would be the safety of the wide sea, cables were severed, anchors were lost, and hulls and rigging were destroyed. When the San Lorenzo, a large vessel, made its way to Calais Bar, Howard personally rifled her, establishing a precedent that may have been unfavourable in the event that more galleons had been engaged.

On the morning of Monday, July 29, the entire Armada was in a pitiful state by the time daybreak arrived. Medina Sidonia's immediate hope was the ignoble one of rescuing his squadrons from total destruction, and it was without formation. Its entire goal had been frustrated beyond remedies, and there was no way to cure the situation. At first, it did not appear that his odds were very good. He had already deployed his ships along the coast between Gravelines and Dunkirk by this point in time. Because of their stronghold at Flushing, the Dutch rebels were able to eliminate any possibility of the Spaniards reaching the safe haven of Antwerp.

A freshening wind was carrying them towards a shelving beach, and it was impossible for them to return down the channel. At this point, a great number of ships were leaking as a result of damage sustained during the battle; food and water were running low since Medina Sidonia, in contrast to Howard, had not been able to re-victual during the intermittent periods of action. Above all else, they were still in the grasp of a determined adversary, and they were in waters that they were well familiar with. For a period of eight hours, the English, under the leadership of Howard and Drake, harassed the Spaniards with their relentless attacks. Despite the fact that they never allowed the Spanish soldiers to board, they succeeded in closing the range.

On the 30th of July, the Spaniards experienced their one and only stroke of good fortune, and it appeared to them as if it were a miracle. Because of the change in wind direction, which went from west-northwest to west-southwest, they were able to steer their ship into the open sea, leaving behind a half dozen wrecks on the Banks of Zealand. Drake wrote to Walsingham in London, "We have them before us, and mind with the Grace of God to wrestle a fall with them." Walsingham was travelling in London at the time. When I saw the enemy flying in the direction of the north, I felt a sense of satisfaction that I had never experienced before. I pray that God would bless you with a good eye towards the Duke of

Parma, since if we are still alive, I have no doubt that you will be able to handle the situation with the Duke of Sidonia in the manner that he will wish for himself... in the midst of his orange trees.'

By the time the adversary's forces reached the latitude of Newcastle-on-Tyne, Howard was forced to abandon the pursuit. It was now too late for him to replenish his supplies; he had used up all of his powder, and the victorious had little chance of keeping up with the battleships that were due to reach Scottish waters. Diseases such as scurvy, dysentery, and typhus were starting to manifest themselves among the crews, and it was becoming increasingly important to return to port as soon as it was possible to do so. Medina Sidonia, who was both brave and dissatisfied, gave the order for his remaining ships to sail across the northern region of Scotland on their route back to Medina Sidonia.

In spite of the fact that it was a lengthy and stormy path, it was at least safer than trying to go back the way they had come. As far as the Orkney Islands, he was under surveillance; nevertheless, when the scouting vessels witnessed the Armada transform into the teeth of a westerly storm, they were aware of the inevitable outcome that must befall it. One unfortunate galleon was later blown so far east that she came ashore off the coast of Bolt Head in Devonshire. Other wrecks occurred in the Outer Hebrides and on the rocky coast of Donegal, Connaught, and Galway. Some of these places were also affected by the storm.

Between the months of July and August, the Armada suffered a total loss of sixty-four ships and at least ten thousand men. This dispersed manner resulted in the loss of around twenty-five warships. It is impossible to adequately convey to your Majesty the difficulties and sufferings that we have endured, as Medina Sidonia wrote in a letter to King Philip. "They have demonstrated a level of excellence that has never been witnessed on any previous voyage." "The words were nothing less than the truth," the speaker said. In order to disperse all of my adversaries, he caused the winds and floods to surge. In a song of thanksgiving, Queen Elizabeth wrote this, and all of her subjects recited it as well. In spite of the fact that winds and waterways had proven to be reliable allies, it was Howard's management of the fleet and the nimble way in which his ships were able to manoeuvre that ensured England would not be successfully invaded.

Despite the fact that the Queen possessed leaders of competence and sailors of resolve, her domain would continue to be untouchable. The naval battle that took place in the waters of the English Channel in 1588, which resulted in the defeat of the Spanish Armada, was a defining moment in the history of Europe. Both England and Spain experienced severe short-term and long-term repercussions as a result of the aftermath of this war, which reshaped the geopolitical environment of the time. In the immediate aftermath of the event, England established itself as the preeminent nuclear power.

As a result of England's triumph over the Spanish Armada, which had a fleet that was thought to be unbeatable, England's nautical prestige was strengthened. This win was not just a military victory, but it was also an important morale booster, strengthening national pride and solidifying the rule of Queen Elizabeth I. The victory enabled England to keep control over the English Channel, which was essential for the country's security and commerce interests. The loss was a crushing blow for Spain, despite their best efforts. The Spanish Navy suffered a loss of ships and service members, which resulted in a reduction in its dominance over the waters of Europe.

When it came to the economy, the defeat was expensive and put a strain on Spain's already overextended treasury. As a result of this loss, Spain's ability to exert effective control over her enormous overseas empire and its influence in European politics both began to erode. The result of the combat had significant repercussions for the overall strategy of the conflict. The beginning of the collapse of Spanish maritime dominance and the beginning of England's ascent to prominence as a significant naval force were both marked by this event. There were huge repercussions for the future of European colonialism and trade as a result of this transfer of naval power.

Because of England's stronger naval position, it was able to challenge Spain's dominance in the Americas and establish the foundation for its own great colonial empire in the years that followed. It is impossible to overestimate the significance of the conflict in the annals of military history. It demonstrated the efficacy of novel naval strategies as well as the significance of weather and topography in the context of naval warfare. Two of the most important reasons that contributed to the outcome were the English employment of fireships to break the Spanish formation and the Armada's vulnerability to the stormy waters of the northern seas.

In conclusion, the defeat of the Spanish Armada had significant and long-lasting repercussions for both Spain and that country, England. It was the beginning of a new era for England, one that would be characterised by naval dominance and colonial expansion. It was the beginning of Spain's gradual loss of maritime and imperial dominance, and it was a significant event for Spain. Throughout the course of naval history, the conflict has left an indelible mark, serving as a symbol of the shift in power dynamics in Europe and the ascent of England to the position of leading naval and colonial power. If the English had not been victorious over the Spanish Armada, it is quite likely that the British Empire would not have existed. Furthermore, if the British Empire had existed, it is highly probable that the United States of America would not have come into being.

15. Trafalgar, 1803 (1st Place)

Nelson had received no backlash following Denmark's ardours. As soon as they learned of the combat, the admiralty passed Parker and placed Nelson in command. It was an undesirable step for him, as he harboured no ill will towards his boss, and his condition was such that he would have preferred to go home had there been no need for more active steps in the Baltic. For once, their Lordships granted his wishes without hesitation, maybe more because they needed his services for a new purpose than just to appease him. He had hardly returned home when he was assigned to command his nation's seaward defences.

His orders were to organise the "sea fencibles" and flotillas, which would be the main defence against any invasion attempt by the Grand Army, which Bonaparte had gathered around Boulogne. The appointment only served to frustrate Nelson, and on August 15, 1801, he launched his one and only attack on Boulogne itself, believing, as did Drake and other great leaders before him, that it would succeed spectacularly. Due to their extensive preparation, the French were able to repel the attack with some casualties. It was Nelson's final service prior to the titanic struggle's brief cessation following the signing of the Treaty of Amiens in May 1802. The Treaty resolved nothing and was only in effect for a single year. It provided a respite for the principal land and sea powers, who were the main players in the war, but when it resumed, Napoleon's massive army remained stationed on the Channel shore, waiting for the day when French sailors would gain control of the sea, if only temporarily, so that it could cross.

The home fleet of Britain remained the cornerstone of its defence strategy. William Cornwallis, whose station lay off the western end of the Channel, was in command of it. As a follower of Hawke, like Nelson, Cornwallis believed in keeping a careful eye on Brest in all weather conditions, and although he was in control of business, the northern area's maritime affairs were in the best hands. Nelson was about to make the French Mediterranean Fleet, based in Toulon, his own permanent object.

The day following the resumption of hostilities, he received the order he would have preferred, and on May 18, he raised his flag in the magnificent three-decker Victory, which had been anchored during the Seven Years' War when he was still a young boy and had previously carried the flags of most of the most prominent admirals of the time. For the rest of his life, he was rarely apart from her. She turned into his majestic residence, worthy of the banner of a man as unwavering in combat as he is in observation. An axiom of Monck, the hero of the Four-Day Battle, that was appropriate for an enterprise was that the two main components of a soldier are courage and suffering; there is equal honour in enduring hardships during a war as there is in engaging in valiant combat and accomplishing great feats.

However, it is simpler to locate men who are eager to give themselves up to death than it is to locate those who will patiently endure labour. Nelson's job now was to work hard and be patient. The campaign that culminated in Trafalgar was a great success, but it started with a protracted stay in the Gulf of Lions and lasted for most of 1803, 1804, and 1805. 'They were tedious, dreary, eventless months,' wrote Admiral Mahan, Nelson's kind American biographer, describing the relentless, silent pressure of Nelson's navy, 'those months of watching and waiting of the large ships before the French arsenals.' These words have since become legendary.

They may have seemed pointless to many, but they rescued England. There has never been a more striking example of how sea power has shaped human history. Nelson rarely had enough ships for the task at hand, but he knew how to make the most of what he had, and finally, his transcendent services had earned him the position he deserved. "Those far distant, storm-beaten ships, upon which the Grand Army never looked," he said, standing between it and the domination of the world. According to St. Vincent, the Mediterranean needed "an officer of splendour." Now she was given one.

As time went on and Spain sided with him in the conflict once more, Napoleon came up with what he thought was a brilliant plan. His blockaded squadrons should escape from Toulon, the ports of Biscay, and Brest. Spanish soldiers from Cartagena and Cadiz should join them, and together the armies will form a massive armada in the West Indies that will dwarf any ambitions Philip of Spain had. With their overwhelming might, the admirals ought to return to Europe and take control of the Straits of Dover. After then, the soldiers should cross at Napoleon's signal. There could be no question about the matter under his dominant genius. The allegedly unconquerable Britain would fall under his vassal rule.

Napoleon treated his sailors like generals, even after his fleet had a bad experience at Aboukir Bay. He paid little attention to potential adversary reactions and made no allowance for the environment in which they operated. Though incorrect, this was normal behaviour from the greatest soldier in history. Nevertheless, there were moments when it appeared as though at least part of his schemes could be successful since, twice in the early months of 1805, his "lucky" Admiral Villeneuve managed to flee Toulon.

The initial attempt failed, and the French returned, ravaged by the weather that Nelson had been dealing with since 1803. Knowing that Villeneuve had escaped, Nelson made a false cast and sailed all the way to Alexandria, fearful that Egypt may again become the object of Bonaparte's aspirations. As he had once before, in 1798, he returned to find the port abandoned, and he was heartbroken. He believed that such an experienced combatant shouldn't have committed that specific error. We learned the lesson well.

When Villeneuve got away a second time, Nelson waited off" Sardinia, and it was there, in a favourite anchorage, that he had the news he most dreaded. Villeneuve had been seen to pass through the Straits of Gibraltar on 8 April - ten days earlier - and it appeared possible that he might have picked up the Spaniards from Cartagena on his way. It was one of the darkest hours in Nelson's life. He had had his fill of 'Sufferance'. Was he to be denied his hour of Valour? It was not until 4 May that Nelson was able to provision off Tetuan, for the winds were foul.

Two days later he anchored off Gibraltar, and he sailed the same evening. His problem was complex, for not only had he to guess the enemy's direction, but he had to give cover to an expeditionary force under General Craig, destined for the

Mediterranean. Having seen Craig safe, and knowing that Cornwallis was in strength to the north, Nelson made for the West Indies.

Again, his luck was out. He made a good passage to Barbados, and would have pushed on to Martinique had not faulty intelligence sent him south to Trinidad. He found nothing. This was all the more mortifying since Nelson himself never believed Trinidad to have been an object of Villeneuve's, but he could not disregard what seemed to be unimpeachable evidence from an army officer with whom he had served before, and in whom he had confidence. Villeneuve, after summoning such Spaniards as were ready at Cadiz, had made his crossing, though his ships were not in the best order. Then, hearing that Nelson was on his heels, instead of waiting for the French Atlantic squadrons which Bonaparte had told him to expect, he sped back to Europe.

Nelson, when he learnt the Frenchman's movements, sent a fast brig direct to England, her captain having orders to warn the Admiralty. The brig actually sighted the Allied fleet on passage, and was thus able to give the latest news to Whitehall. Nelson returned to Gibraltar, a bitterly disappointed man. He had leave to return home, and made use of the chance taking with him the Superb which needed docking. Lord Barham head of the Admiralty order a strong fleet to be assembled under Sir Robert Calders to intercept the combined fleet. Nelson after anchoring at Spithead spent nearly a month at his home in Merton, London.

Because Villeneuve had escaped capture at the battle of the Nile some saw it as less than a complete victory such were the high expectations on the Royal Navy at this time. The French who, ever since the Nile, had studied Nelson's character and methods with the fascinated attention which was their due. 'One day,' said Captain Keats of the Superb, 'walking with Lord Nelson in the grounds at Merton, talking of naval affairs, he said to me: "No day can be long enough to arrange a couple of Fleets and fight a decisive battle, according to the old system. I'll tell you how I'm going to combat them when we meet them, which is when I was supposed to have been with him. "With the remaining part of the fleet formed in two lines, I shall go at them at once, if I can, about one third of their line from the leading ship," he said. "I shall form the Fleet into three Divisions in three lines.

One Division shall be composed of twelve or fourteen of the fastest two-decked ships, while I shall always keep to windward, or in a situation of advantage; and I shall put them under an officer who, I am sure, will employ them in the manner I wish, if possible." "I consider it.I paused, feeling that such a matter demanded careful thought. He saw it and replied, "But I'll tell you what / think of it." It will, in my opinion, surprise and confuse the adversary. They won't understand who I am. It will bring forward a pellmell battle, and that is what I want." '

That, indeed, was not only the core of the matter - but Keats had caught something of Nelson's infectious enthusiasm. The Superb could not be ready in time, Keats missed the battle, and Nelson would not have enough ships to form his flying division, but the mode of attack held good, even to the element of surprise. Villeneuve, though he knew, wrote that Nelson 'will not trouble to form a line parallel to our own and fight it out with the gun... he will try to double our rear, cut through the line, and bring against the ships thus isolated, groups of his own to surround and capture them', did not know all the details of Nelson's idea, which was so daring, tactically, so unlike anything that had gone before, and which would be so inappropriate as a model for lesser leaders that it could be regarded as a plan to succeed only once, under particular circumstances, and with a fleet incontestably superior not in numbers but in fortitude, gunnery, seamanship, and training.

The Ferrol joined the fleet off" Cadiz on 28 September, and Nelson infused it with a new zeal. "I got the sweetest feeling of my life from the reception I received," he stated. "I think everyone was very happy to see me," he continued....and it was as shocking as an electric jolt when I tried to describe the "Nelson touch"—his scheme. All of them agreed as some cried. The admirals on down reiterated, "It must succeed, if ever they will allow us to get at them! "A few of the more seasoned captains did not think the Combined Fleet would leave port. "It was new; it was singular; it was simple! " Given the late season, Villeneuve might very well spend the entire winter comfortably.

Nelson was of the opinion that it would turn out differently, and Napoleon took advantage of this by first telling Villeneuve to head for the Mediterranean at the earliest possible moment and then sending another Admiral to take his place. Napoleon believed that Villeneuve had run out of luck and that his extravagant plans for invasion were undoubtedly coming to an end. He had another plan for his soldiers. Marching it to the centre of the Continent, he would add fresh triumphs to the numerous ones he had already achieved. Following Nelson's allocation of several weeks to assemble his fleet, Blackwood sent out a warning from the ship Euryalus on October 19 that the enemy was advancing. In the lead-up to his sortie, Villeneuve had given the order for a portion of his force to drive Blackwood and the inshore squadron out of the way, while Nelson maintained his main force well out of sight.

Villeneuve had no choice but to sail his entire force because the French maneuver had failed and the ships involved in the operation were unable to return. Although he was unaware of Nelson's precise fleet count, which stood at twenty-seven-line ships, he had thirty-three of his own, fifteen of which were Spanish, and he felt that with that kind of might, he ought to be able to execute his master's orders. Nelson was far out to sea when he received word that the enemy was stirring. In an attempt to prevent Villeneuve from reaching the Mediterranean, he gave the order for his ships to head for the Straits of Gibraltar. Now he knew exactly where he was going. A French admiral should never have travelled north at this time of year.

During the night of October 19 and the day and night that followed, there was a lot of maneuvering going on. Villeneuve was trying, though not very successfully, to get his ships in the right order, and Nelson was keeping his main strength hidden so that his opponent would have to commit himself completely to trying to get to the mouth of the Straits. On October 21, the Fleets were visible to one another at first light, with Villeneuve continuing to travel south. Nelson gave the order for his ships to position themselves as before, with Collingwood directing the leeward column and him leading the windward. Only mild winds prevailed, with a westward swell portending a storm; nevertheless, the wind direction was more to the north than west, contrary to Nelson's expectations.

Villeneuve turned around as early as eight o'clock. Nelson would have expected this action, since the Combined Fleet could not pass Gibraltar without fighting, and Villeneuve's best option was to retreat to Cadiz, where, should a full-scale conflict be unavoidable, at least he could repair his damage. Calling the frigate captains to the Victory, they were to get their orders. All they meant to say was that the rear ships were to move as fast and as well as they could, regardless of the official 'Order of Sailing' that Nelson had drafted. "We scrambled into battle as best we could," one of the captains subsequently remarked, a statement that would have terrified most previous commanders-in-chief as well as that precise tactician Lord Howe.

The admiral then made his way around the Victory, complimenting all of Hardy's planning and inspiring the crew. Three French emigrants and seventy-one foreigners of almost every country, including twenty-two Americans, made up a sizeable share of the volunteers! once he had personally witnessed everything. When Nelson went to his cabin to retire, signal lieutenant Pasco discovered him on his knees. He was dedicating a prayer to his personal journal, which is now a treasure trove of the English language: '. ...."May the Great God, whom I worship, grant a great and glorious Victory to my country and to Europe in general; and may no misconduct in any one tarnish it; and may humanity after Victory be the predominant feature in the British Fleet," Nelson wrote. I personally dedicate my life to the One who created me, and I pray for His guidance as I strive to sincerely serve my nation. I give up myself to Him, as well as the righteous cause that He has given me to stand up for. Indeed. Indeed. Amen.'

When Nelson got up to the upper deck, he told Blackwood that, in his view, everyone knew exactly what they were talking about. Nelson, however, stuck to his beliefs. Around a quarter to noon, His Lordship approached me on the poop and said, "I wish to say to the Fleet, England confides THAT EVERY MAN WILL DO HIS DUTY." He also said, "You must be quick, because I have one more to make, which is for close action." Pasco related this story. I responded: "If your lordship will permit me to substitute expects for confides, the signal will soon be completed, because the word 'expect' is in the vocabulary, and 'confides' must be spelt". "That will do, Pasco, make it directly," Nelson quickly and seemed satisfied.

As a result, the Fleet moved into action, and Collingwood, not alone in his complaint, expressed his wish that his old buddy would cease signalling because they all knew their business sufficiently. One of the numerous ways that Trafalgar differed from previous major naval engagements was that Nelson led the Victory and Collingwood led the Royal Sovereign. Around twelve o'clock, Collingwood was the first to go into battle. He fought by himself for a while, feeling as though it would never end. Nelson remarked, 'Look at how that fine fellow Collingwood puts his ship into motion!' The magnificent three-decker proved impressive to both friends and foes thanks to its expert handling.

The combined fleet was soon under attack from Collingwood's. Everything proceeded as expected. The enemy line was breached as planned by Nelson; their leading ships were unable to assist those in need until an unconventional battle of the sailing era was fought, burning through the autumn afternoon and reducing the Combined Fleet of France and Spain to complete disarray.

At approximately 1:15 p.m., Hardy, Nelson was hit by a bullet fired from the Redoutale, piercing his shoulder. Nelson said, "My back is shot through! " In order to keep the ship's company from losing heart, Sergeant Seeker of the Marines and a group of sailors brought him downstairs to the cockpit while covering his face with a handkerchief. Nelson lived for a further three hours in excruciating pain, but he lived to hear Hardy deliver the news he had been waiting for: that the battle had been won.

Many enemy soldiers had lost their lives. Collingwood then destroyed the allied rearguard, Villeveuve himself, and all of his staff became prisoners of war. Villeveuve's own life had served its objective of preventing interference with Collingwood. and every member of his staff were POWs.

Having fulfilled his obligations, as he frequently remarked to himself, and happily in his final hours. Nelson may pass away contentedly, at the moment of his greatest fulfilment. He had accomplished the goal for which he had lived, and there was never a need or opportunity for another large-scale naval conflict during the remaining years of the war with France. The British navy maintained its dominant position for over a century after effectively, if not quite, wiping out the adversary.

The line that describes Nelson's death in the log of the Victory is the most straightforward, comprehensive, and formal of all the records of his passing. "Partially firing continued until 4.30," the record states. "After reporting a victory to Commander-in-Chief and Right Honourable Lord Viscount Nelson KB, he then succumbed to his wounds." As great as the victory was, following the war, Gibraltar received only four prizes. As Nelson had anticipated, a storm materialised, and the defeated forces found it challenging to salvage their own vessels.

It meant very little in the long term. All future scholars of war would remember and honour Nelson's brilliance and example, and Collingwood would carry on the task he had begun with his buddy. In remarks that emerged from knowledge spanning the majority of Nelson's maritime career,

Collingwood wrote: "Lord Nelson is an incomparable man, a blessing to any country that is engaged in such a war." With ideas of the Nile and Copenhagen in mind, Collingwood wrote, "An enemy that commits a false step in his view is ruined, and it comes on him with an impetuosity that allows him no time to recover." His remarks foretold Nelson's final conflict, in which he himself played such a magnificent role.

The fallout from the October 21, 1805, Battle of Trafalgar had a significant and long-lasting impact on both naval combat and the larger geopolitical environment of the era. This pivotal battle, which took place during the Napoleonic Wars, not only changed the direction of the war but also the balance of naval power in Europe.

The British Royal Navy became the undisputed king of the seas in the short aftermath. Admiral Horatio Nelson, who sadly lost his life in the conflict, led the triumph at Trafalgar, which put an end to any real threat to British naval dominance for more than a century. Because of Britain's superiority, it was able to put France under a naval blockade, which severely hindered Napoleon's capacity to project military force abroad and hampered his economic ambitions. France and her allies suffered a terrible defeat. During the Napoleonic era, the French Navy never fully recovered from the loss of ships and experienced sailors.

Napoleon was much more focused on his ground wars in Europe as a result of this disaster, which severely curtailed his intentions to invade Britain. An era of British dominance in maritime trade and colonial development followed the conflict, which effectively put an end to French hopes to challenge British naval supremacy. The result of Trafalgar had a big impact on the economy. Due to its dominance of international trade routes and maritime dominance, Britain was able to expand its empire and its economic might on a worldwide scale. The incapacity of France to defend its colonies and trade channels resulted in economic distress and added to the financial issues that beset Napoleon's government.

Trafalgar had long-term strategic effects on European geopolitics. It made certain that the Napoleonic Wars would take place mostly on land, where Napoleon had greater success. Napoleon was able to win some land battles, but due to Britain's superior naval might, he was never able to completely vanquish the British, who kept up their disruption of French trade and assistance of his adversaries. The Battle of Trafalgar holds great significance in military history due to its tactical genius, especially to Nelson's creative tactics.

As naval warfare evolved in the 19th century, it also signaled the end of a period of extensive fleet conflicts with wooden sailing ships. In summary, all parties involved in the Battle of Trafalgar suffered significant repercussions. It was a turning point in naval warfare history that cemented British naval supremacy, altered European geopolitics, and had enormous economic ramifications. Trafalgar Square is a well-known landmark in London, with a statue of Lord Nelson perched atop of Nelson's column, the square's centerpiece. Most of the world great cities lay on their coastlines, he who commands the oceans can go where he pleases, lay siege to great fortresses and cities, and dominate the world. Such was the world of Horatio Lord Nelson, and the world that he created for the British Empire for 100 years following the Battle of Trafalgar.

AUTHORS EPILOGUE

As we reach the conclusion of "Greatest Naval Battles in History," it is imperative to reflect on the monumental role naval power has played throughout the centuries. This book, crafted with the intent to enlighten both the young and the inquisitively minded of today, has journeyed through the tumultuous seas of history, showcasing battles that not only shaped the fate of nations but also the course of our world.

Naval power, often the silent arbiter of historical tides, has been a crucial factor in the rise and fall of empires. From the triremes of ancient Greece to the mighty battleships of the 20th century, the ability to project power across the vast, unpredictable oceans has been a defining element in establishing dominance. The age of colonialism, a period marked by the expansion of European powers across the globe, was fundamentally underpinned by naval supremacy. Control of the seas meant not just military might, but also the ability to control trade routes, colonize distant lands, and exert influence far from home shores.

Throughout this book, we have seen how battles like the Spanish Armada in 1588, Trafalgar in 1805, and Midway in 1942, among others, were not just clashes of ships and sailors, but pivotal moments that reshaped borders and ideologies. These battles, fought across different eras, underpin the narrative of naval strategy and its evolution. They highlight the ingenuity, bravery, and sometimes the hubris of those who sought to rule the waves.

While some readers may have different views on the battles chosen or the interpretations presented, this book aims to provide a concise, yet comprehensive understanding of naval warfare's impact on history. It is a tribute to those who braved the unforgiving seas, whether in wooden ships or steel behemoths, and a reminder of the strategic importance of naval power.

In today's era, where information is instantaneous and the past can seem distant, it is essential to remember these battles and their outcomes. They are not just stories or dates in a history book; they are the chapters of human endeavour, ambition, and sometimes tragedy, that have shaped the world we live in.

As we close this chapter on naval history, let us carry forward the lessons and legacies of these great battles, understanding that the sea is not just a part of our geography but a significant canvas of our shared human history.

Bibliography

"The Influence of Sea Power Upon History, 1660-1783" by Alfred Thayer Mahan (1890)

"Naval Warfare in the Age of Sail: War at Sea 1756–1815" by Bernard Ireland (2000)

"Six Frigates: The Epic History of the Founding of the U.S. Navy" by Ian W. Toll (2006)

"The Price of Admiralty: The Evolution of Naval Warfare" by John Keegan (1988)

"Fleet Tactics and Naval Operations" by Wayne P. Hughes Jr. and Robert Girrier (Third Edition, 2018)

"Sea power: A Guide for the Twenty-First Century" by Geoffrey Till (Fourth Edition, 2018)

"The Command of the Ocean: A Naval History of Britain, 1649-1815" by N.A.M. Rodger (2004)

"Castles of Steel: Britain, Germany, and the Winning of the Great War at Sea" by Robert K. Massie (2003)

"The Battle of Midway" by Craig L. Symonds (2011)

"The War for All the Oceans: From Nelson at the Nile to Napoleon at Waterloo" by Roy Adkins and Lesley Adkins (2007)

"The Age of the Ship of the Line: The British and French Navies, 1650-1815" by Jonathan R. Dull (2009)

"Empires of the Sea: The Siege of Malta, the Battle of Lepanto, and the Contest for the Centre of the World" by Roger Crowley (2008)

Printed in Great Britain
by Amazon